TEDDY SUHREN: ACE OF ACES

TEDDY SUHREN: ACE OF ACES

Memoirs of a U-Boat Rebel

Teddy Suhren & Fritz Brustat-Naval

Translated by Frank James

Greenhill Books

Teddy Suhren: Ace of Aces

This paperback edition published in 2025 by Greenhill Books
c/o Pen & Swords Books Limited,
George House, Unit 12 & 13, Beevor Street,
Off Pontefract Road, Barnsley, South Yorkshire S71 1HN
www.greenhillbooks.com

Paperback edition: 978-1-80500-190-4
ePub edition: 978-1-80500-211-6
PDF: 978-1-80500-212-3

Publishing history
Teddy Suhren: Ace of Aces was first published in Germany as *Nasses Eichlenlaub* by Koehlers Verlagsgellschaft in 1983. It was first published in English by Chatham Publishing, an imprint of Greenhill Books, London, in 2006, and by Frontline Books, an imprint of Pen & Sword Books Ltd, in 2011 (hardback edition) and 2017 (paperback edition). This edition, published by Greenhill Books, London, in 2025, includes a new Introduction by Lawrence Paterson.

A CIP data record for this title is available from the British Library

Printed and bound in England by
CPI Group (UK) Ltd, Croydon, CR0 4YY

FSC www.fsc.org MIX Paper | Supporting responsible forestry FSC® C013604

Contents

List of Ranks

Kriegsmarine
Großadmiral = Admiral of the Fleet
Admiral = Admiral
Kommodore = Commodore
Kapitän-zur-See = Captain
Fregattenkapitän = 'Captain (junior)'
Korvettenkapitän = Commander
Kapitänleutnant ('Kaleu')= Lieutenant Commander
Oberleutnant zur See = Lieutenant
Leutnant zur See = Sub-Lieutenant
Oberfähnrich zur See = Senior Midshipman
Fähnrich zur See = Midshipman
Obersteuermann = Chief Quartermaster
Oberbootsmann = Boatswain
Bootsmaat = Boatswain's mate

Others
Generalfeldmarschall = Field Marshal

Glossary

Abwehr = German Military Intelligence
BdU = Befehlshaber der Unterseeboote = Commander of U-Boats
FdU = Führer der Unterseeboote = Leader of U-Boats
'Kaleu' = short for 'Kapitänleutnant'
KC = Knight's Cross
KK = Korvettenkapitän
LI = Chief Engineer
OdM = Oberbefehlshaber der Marine = Commander-in-Chief of the Navy
PK = Propagandakompanie = War reporters and photographers
SD = Sicherheitdienst = SS intelligence and security police
'Stürkorl' = slang for Obersteuermann
ULD = Submarine Training Division
WO = Watch Officer: 1WO therefore is 1st Watch Officer, *ie* First Lieutenant

Introduction

EVERYBODY HAD A STORY to tell about Teddy. That was what struck me the most about this remarkable man while researching my own book about his time as captain of *U-564*. Over the course of many interviews with German veterans of the U-boat service, Reinhard 'Teddy' Suhren's name was one that came up time and time again, usually accompanied with laughter at the recollection of some real or perceived misdemeanour that he had committed. For, within a naval service that prided itself on tradition, he was in many ways a true maverick.

While it is fair to say that Dönitz's U-boat men were given much greater leeway in their behaviour than the personnel of other branches of the Kriegsmarine, Teddy Suhren managed to push even those boundaries on more than one occasion. Possessed of a wicked sense of humour, tempered by a keen intelligence and genuine aptitude for his chosen career as a U-boat officer, Suhren carved an unforgettable niche within a service whose mystique remains long after the last few surviving veterans have passed away. Somewhat ironically, it is not his particularly impressive military accomplishments that was usually the main topic of conversation, but his off-duty demeanour and unforgettable personality that loomed larger than his relatively modest physique.

Teddy Suhren was, and remains, almost larger than life to men who shared his U-boat experience. For example, a conversation with the former radio operator of *U-604*, Georg Seitz, in his home near Mannheim, yielded tales about Suhren's somewhat risky humorous remarks at the expense of the Nazis. Meanwhile, discussion with Erich Topp, the 'Ace' former commander of *U-552* among other boats, included amusing stories from his and Teddy's adventurous visit to Obersalzberg and personal encounters with Martin Bormann, Eva Braun and Adolf Hitler. Teddy had been investigated by the Abwehr for consorting with a Jewish woman and 'drinking raucously' with a black African man in a Hamburg bar. At the end of one war patrol, he jokingly ordered his U-boat back out to sea after enquiring of the gathered welcoming committee whether the Nazis were still in charge and being assured that they were. Fortunately, his commanding officers of the U-boat arm staunchly defended their wayward charge.

Reinhard 'Teddy' Suhren became an almost legendary figure amongst the men of the Kriegsmarine's U-boat service. On the outside he seems an oddly atypical U-boat officer, with his irreverent sense of humour and a seemingly natural distrust of authority that would periodically make him the bane of his superiors. Suhren held a steadfast devotion and loyalty to his commander, Karl Dönitz, which was reciprocated in turn throughout his wartime career. In reality, there was far more to Suhren than the legend would lead you to believe. He was a member of the Wehrmacht's officer corps and, as such, was imbued with the sense of tradition and honour with which it was accompanied. A largely apolitical man, he nonetheless held a sense of national patriotism that you would expect of that time and era, regardless of which government was heading the nation.

The U-boats of the Second World War still hold a particular fascination for many people – sometimes far in excess of their actual achievements – and they are often portrayed within popular media in lurid ways that bear little or no resemblance to reality. For example, Jonathan Mostow's appalling film *U-571,* released in 2000, does genuine disservice to the British servicemen who recovered the first working Enigma machine, as well as those who died recovering Enigma parts on other occasions. It also showed the crew of a U-boat unquestioningly machine-gunning survivors of a merchant ship they had sunk. To showcase the obviously fictional story, Mostow could just have easily used the number of a boat never commissioned into the Kriegsmarine. Instead, the survivors of the real *U-571* were justifiably upset.

Accounts and histories of the war within the Atlantic, as well as the more expansive campaigns in which U-boats fought, continue to be written. Reinhard Suhren was one of those fortunate U-boat officers who served throughout the entire war, though he was lucky to leave the frontlines in October 1942. He had begun the war as First Watch Officer (IWO) of *U-48*, the most successful U-boat of the entire war. As IWO, his responsibilities included deck gunnery and surfaced torpedo firing. Suhren soon proved to be an exceptional torpedo shot, evidenced by his award of the Knight's Cross in November 1940 while aboard *U-48*. In this role, under three different captains, he was responsible for all surface torpedo shooting. His was the first Knight's Cross awarded by the U-boat service to anyone other than a captain.

Sadly, it was Teddy who fired the torpedo that sank SS *City of Benares*; an accident of war and a tragically inevitable result of mercantile convoy war in which 258 people were killed, including 77 out of 90 children being evacuated from Britain to escape the Luftwaffe bombing. The sinking of this ship contributed to the subsequent nervous breakdown of its captain, Heinrich Bleichrodt, and troubled Teddy for the rest of his life according to his widow Hannelore. It may seem somewhat strange that this particular event evoked such strong emotions among many of the *U-48* crewmen, but, like bomber crews of all nations that attacked relatively 'faceless' targets, there was perhaps a certain amount of detachment to sinking enemy ships. A tonnage war, such as was waged by German U-boats, pivoted solely on the accrued tonnage of enemy merchant shipping being sunk; not the inflicting of casualties. That, however, is the tragic reality for both antagonists of such a war, resulting in burning ships, terrified passengers and crews and the loss of lives in the expanse of the mid-Atlantic.

In April 1941, Suhren took command of the new Type VIIC *U-564*, mounting six war patrols as far afield as the Caribbean Sea and adding the Oak Leaves to his Knight's Cross. As was Dönitz's custom for those men who had been at sea since the war's beginning, the experienced Suhren was then moved ashore to pass on his knowledge and skills in training establishments, ending the war as the commander of U-boats in Northern Norway. This latter experience was extremely sobering for the veteran officer as he was in no doubt as to the probable outcome of the war, yet duty bound to continue fighting to the end.

By this time, the U-boat service must have seemed barely recognisable to someone like Teddy Suhren. Commanders were younger and less experienced, unable to attain mastery of their new role within the extensive service as watch officer or 'commander-in-training' aboard combat boats that the early war years had provided. Losses had always been heavy within Dönitz's U-boats from the outset of hostilities, but by 1944, the life expectancy of a U-boat crew had reached its lowest ebb; 249 U-boats lost during that year alone. Despite being forced in his new role to deal with difficult officers either more politically motivated or of higher rank and of no mind to cooperate with him, he made the best of a difficult situation both logistically and militarily. He was a man whose previously rebellious reputation often preceded him, yet he retained a strong sense of loyalty both to and from those men under his command.

The end of the war found Teddy incarcerated in Oslo by British authorities, potentially held as a witness for the impending trials to be held in Nuremberg. Though this never came to pass, Suhren saw up close within his fellow prisoners the frequent conversion of formerly devout National Socialist officers to born-again Christians and flag bearers for democracy. He was unimpressed.

After release from imprisonment, Teddy learned of the tragic death of his father, mother and sister in the distant Sudetenland. Cornered by an angry mob of 'partisans' in the final days of the war, Geert Suhren killed his wife, daughter and then himself rather than let them be subjected to what would likely have been a more brutal and prolonged end. Suhren returned to a shattered Germany and began to rebuild his life. His first wife had since deserted him and taken up with an American officer, which shook him badly. Nonetheless, he began a successful career in the oil merchant shipping industry, beginning with the broken shell of a company and successfully steering it to prosperity. Though he refused repeated requests to join the Bundeswehr due to his objections at the perceived criminalisation of Wehrmacht veterans, he became a leading figure within the U-boat veterans' organisations and founding chairman of the German Naval Association (Deutscher Marinebund), an umbrella organisation for all naval associations and naval fraternities. As such he was the key speaker at the first post-war naval veteran meeting in Hamburg in 1954, during which he strongly lamented the continued incarceration of Grossadmirals Raeder and Dönitz and continuing criminalisation of German veterans.

He died 25 August 1984 of stomach cancer. Teddy had married for the second time, and I was personally fortunate enough to spend many hours with his widow Hannelore and daughter Gesa in the former's Hamburg flat, listening to fascinating stories from both their and Teddy's lives. The insight that I gained into this enigmatic man widened my perception of exactly who he was, and this book that he co-authored with Fritz Brustat-Naval, also an experienced seaman and former supply ship captain from the Second World War, tells his story perfectly. There is no better way to read of this man's life than through his own words.

Sadly, the veterans of this tumultuous war have nearly all gone now. The more that their personal histories are written down and published, the greater our understanding of not only their own individual experiences, but that of a world torn apart by a conflict greater than that ever seen before. This book tells the story of Reinhard 'Teddy' Suhren's war and his life on either side of it. His name has become legendary, and you will frequently see him mentioned in other books dealing with aspects of the U-boat service, not only because of his extraordinary military accomplishments, but because everybody had a story to tell about Teddy.

Lawrence Paterson, 2025

Translator's Preface

THIS TRANSLATION OF REINHARD ('Teddy') Suhren's memoirs (entitled in the original German *Nasses Eichenlaub* ('Wet Oak Leaves')) was the by-product of researching a fascinating collection of 362 photographs taken on Suhren's last patrol with *U-564* in 1942; most of this collection, which 'surfaced' in Yorkshire in 2000, has now been reproduced in *U-Boat War Patrol*, with an excellent and comprehensive accompanying narrative by Lawrence Paterson. I am grateful to him and Sarah for their company on a whistle-stop tour of Germany, and for checking the typescript of this book for U-boat terminology; to Gudmundur Helgason of uboat.net and all its many and knowledgeable forum participants for parting with so much helpful information; to Debbie Corner of the RN Submarine Museum's photographic archive, where the photos now reside, for permission to use some of her scans of the originals; to Erich Topp for welcoming us so warmly in his home in Remagen and finding time to talk about his wartime experiences; to the Zweibrücken Marinekameradschaft in Niederauerbach, which still bears 'Teddy' Suhren's name, for their continuing friendship and hospitality, and in particular to Dietmar Hoefert and Helmut Herzig for making scans of so much of their own 'Teddy' Suhren Archive for Lawrence and myself; to Horst Bredow of the U-Boat Archiv in Cuxhaven for allowing us to access his unique collection of material; to my old friend Ian Popely – a much better German speaker than myself – for checking the translation for linguistic howlers; to Rob Gardiner and all those at Chatham Publishing for making the whole process of publication so painless; and to my long-suffering wife for her patience while this book has been in the making. Acknowledgement must also be made to Fritz Brustat-Naval, who conducted the interviews with 'Teddy' Suhren in the early 1980s on which the original *Nasses Eichenlaub* was based. The illustrations used here, many of which appeared in the original *Nasses Eichenlaub*, have come from a variety of sources; all reasonable effort has been made to obtain permissions but if there has been any unwitting infringement of copyright I can only apologise, as indeed for any inaccuracies or misinterpretations in the text, for which ultimately I must take responsibility. Finally, I should like to dedicate this book to 'Teddy' Suhren's widow, Frau Hannelore Suhren, and her daughter Gesa; without their warm welcome, their enthusiasm and their encouragement it would never have reached the shelf.

1

Battleships and the GRÖFAZ – How long would the war last?

WE BEGIN IN SPRING 1941. In the naval base on the Baltic then known as Gotenhafen [now Gdynia in Poland] lay what were in their day the two biggest battleships in the world: the *Bismarck* and her sister-ship the *Tirpitz*. With an overall length of 251m [823ft] and beam of 36m [118ft], these giants had a displacement of 41,700 tons. Their heavy armament, twin guns mounted in four turrets, was of 38.1cm [15in] calibre and had a range of around 36kms [22 miles]; each shell weighed 798 kilos [1,760lbs]. Where they struck, no grass

Hitler inspects troops at the launch of the *Tirpitz*.

The majestic *Bismarck* at Kiel.

grew again. The ships' armour plating, made from Krupps steel up to 320mm [12.5in] thick, made them virtually indestructible. They amounted at the time not just to the biggest but also to the most powerful ships of any navy in the world, and were just about invincible. In a word, they were floating fortresses. Their threat was increased by their ability to cruise from their base at 30 knots, driven by 150,000HP and three screws, and to operate over an area of sea as far as South America and back. In strategic terms they were intended for an ocean-going role, to intercept the enemy's merchant shipping in the Atlantic.

There were clear signs of the *Bismarck*'s imminent departure. Rumours were confirmed when on 12 May 1941 Adolf Hitler paid a visit to the battleship, anchored at the Gotenhafen base, where the whole ship's company of 2,300 men were drawn up on parade to welcome him. Perhaps he too just wanted to look at the beautiful lines of the great warship from close-to, and thus inevitably triggered speculation.

After Adolf Hitler and his staff had inspected the *Bismarck*, a joint tea was laid on with the officers of both battleships on

Hitler visits the first of the new generation of U-boats to be built in 1935.

board the *Tirpitz*, which was lying at the quayside. All the Knight's Cross winners in the area of Danzig [now Gdansk] and Gotenhafen had been invited along as what one might call 'window-dressing', including myself, Reinhard Suhren, and my brother Gerd. I was at that time just twenty-five years old, Oberleutnant zur See and Captain of *U-564*, still a new boat. Afterwards we were due to report to the AGRU-front [Ausbildungsgruppe für Front U-Boat – a training unit] at Hella, where my elder brother Gerd, Kapitänleutnant and Ingenieur Offizier, was stationed, to prepare to go to the Front.

There was no red-carpet treatment aboard the *Tirpitz*: just the Führer's standard flying at the top of the mast. The party which assembled at the tea-table under the upper deck numbered about fifty people. In keeping with the character of a warship, all flammable materials were strictly excluded; it was positively spartan in its simplicity, and plain in a military fashion. The only luxury was the white table-cloth. Nazi emblems were totally absent. I noticed that the supreme commander of the navy, Großadmiral Raeder, was not there. That was unusual, but perhaps intentional in order to play down the significance of the visit. To the right and left of Hitler sat the squadron commander, Admiral Lütjens, and the two captains, Kapitäns zur See Lindemann and Topp. I had made the acquaintance of Lütjens already as head of the 1st Destroyer Division; a silent and dry character, he didn't exactly give the impression of a German Nelson.

I sat diagonally across from Hitler. With his hair coming down across his forehead and his little moustache he looked like his photograph to a T. He seemed very relaxed, almost cheerful, and moreover had every reason for it. Poland was overrun, France defeated. We stood firm in the Atlantic, and had joined the Soviet Union in a non-aggression pact. There was only England left. After an introductory exchange of words lasting perhaps ten minutes, Hitler monopolised the conversation; everyone else just listened to him. Adolf, with that guttural and heavily-accented voice which was well-known from the radio, surprised everybody by giving a lecture on armaments and armour-plating, and about the destructive power and capabilities of the world-war fleets, in a way which left even the staff-officers of the battleships standing. And what he said was to the point, there's no denying it. When he came to speak of calibres, he immediately reduced them all to complete silence. What he said was something like this: 'At the time when the *Scharnhorst* and the *Gneisenau* were built, it was explained to me that 28cm (11in) artillery generally speaking were the best one could have; they allowed a rapid rate of fire, with shells which are as effective against the target as those of larger calibre. And yet here on these battleships, here we suddenly have 38cm (15in) cannon. So, what's the point of this, gentlemen?'; and that was about the only opportunity he gave them to utter a single word. There they sat in silence, however, the chief of the fleet, the captains of the two biggest battleships in the world, and all the high-rankers and top-brass present; and they let him do the talking. Surely he ought to

Some of the crew of the *Scharnhorst*: compare the size of the crew of *U-564* on the following page.

have put some more questions to them to entice them out of their reticence: 'How should the war at sea be continued? What's your opinion?' Nothing from the lot of them. Only one person did the talking here: Adolf Hitler. And despite the fact that it was only in irony that Metternich in 1812, when talking about the defeated Napoleon, called him 'the greatest strategist of our century', Adolf had already in our time become known as the 'GRÖFAZ', 'The Greatest Commander of All Time', and one was well-advised not to interrupt, far less contradict him. So in the end it finished up as a proper 'Führer's speech'. When he finished up by going so far as to claim that we would be constructing shipyards in Norway and building ships such as the world had never seen, everyone seemed delighted. After the tea we Knight's Cross holders were presented to Hitler in the Captain's cabin. He was surprised when the name 'Suhren' came up twice, pointed at us and looked questioningly at me. I just said 'We're brothers'. That was that, and we were dismissed.

In contrast to my distinguished brother I remained silent and wrapped up in my own thoughts, so that in the end he rather reproachfully remarked to me, 'Do you know, I have the feeling you've not been enjoying yourself. Come on, think about it, we've just been introduced to the Führer, and that in itself is an exceptional honour . . .' and so on. My reply took a bit longer. 'Sure, that's certainly something which doesn't happen every day, and in one sense I'm delighted. But looking at what has happened so far, I notice that the Führer is just about the only one to have spoken, and then about the kind of details which at the end of the day are not his business; that's what he has a naval staff for. Of course he has managed to convince our lords and masters that he is not an idiot – as with the question about calibre, for example. But is that necessary? Does he need to be concerned with all these matters? Surely someone of his stature cannot try to know so much without dissipating his energies. I don't get it'.

'That's exactly it', my brother interjected. 'The Führer has a phenomenal memory and is interested in everything'. 'That

The crew of *U-564*.

may be so,' I continued. 'You've certainly travelled with him on the motor-yacht the *Grille* and have seen more of him there than I have; perhaps you just know him better. I would have preferred it if things had gone differently, and he'd built up a picture from the comments of the others. They never opened their mouths. And another thing', I added: 'what did he mean by these "ships such as the world has never seen" that he is going to have built – despite the fact that he already has the two biggest battleships? When are they going to be ready for action? In other words, how long is the war to continue? Two years have already passed.'

My brother begged me to be quiet, but once on the train I spoke up again. 'At the end of the day I'm only a simple seaman, and there's a lot I don't know. But I can count up to three, and pick up the odd thing here and there. Look at our invasion of Poland. That affects Russia, and means sooner or later war with the Soviet Union. The troops aren't stationed there for nothing'.

Although so much time has passed, I can picture the scene perfectly today. It took place in May 1941, when the world still seemed to many of us to be pretty well OK. But within the next month Hitler began out of the blue to attack the Soviet Union, and with that the war began to run into difficulties; and four more years were to drag on. That was something no one could have predicted – and even fewer could have predicted what we would have to go through. I myself, a young Oberleutnant, awarded the Knight's Cross for my 'decisive part in sinking 200,000 tons of enemy shipping', was to be twice promoted out of turn 'for exceptional valour against the enemy,' and at twenty-eight was the youngest Fregattenkapitän in the German Navy – and, with 'the Swords to the Oak Leaves to the Knight's Cross' one of the most highly-decorated naval officers anywhere.

As for the battleships with which I began my memoirs, they were to fall victim to the war despite their apparent invincibility. All the rumours about the *Bismarck* were confirmed; in the end shortly after the Führer's visit she cruised off into the Atlantic and only a few days later was lost, complete with Admiral Lütjens.

In the eyes of a young man who still dreamt of sea-battles, the impression produced by these armour-plated giants was grandiose and imposing in the extreme. But the way things turned out, it did not fall to my lot to serve on these big ships, with their parade-ground orders, and divisions by company in which the individual is subordinated to the mass. Once I'd set foot on the narrow deck of a submarine, I instantly fell for their entirely different atmosphere, with their close interdependency between the men. Above all, in the face of all the machinery of war and all the formality of the services, in the foreground stood Man with all his human qualities.

I was always known as 'Teddy' Suhren. God knows, the nickname wasn't intended to be much of a compliment. On the contrary, in the early years I blotted my copy-book many times, and took as much stick as they could give me. That too I'll explain properly later; indeed my meteoric career looked at first as though it was headed rapidly downhill.

2

Why Teddy? – Family destinies – Recruit and Cadet – A cousin in Samoa

To dwell on my nickname 'Teddy' for a moment. In the last summer holidays before my final school exams I was able to take part in a sailing course in Neustadt/Holstein, although the cost involved was not easily affordable by my parents. I had already done some sailing previously, and hoped to improve my skills. To my disappointment pre-military training predominated in the school. Still, since I'd already applied as a potential officer in the Navy, and acceptance, as they impressed on me, actually depended on this cadet-training, we had to put up with it for good or ill. My appearance in this connection however caused some amusement. One day the man in the rank behind me burst into roars of laughter – 'My goodness, Reinhard, your marching makes you look just like a Teddy bear!' It was really poking fun at the figure I cut, and I found it at first far from funny. I didn't think much of marching anyway. Later, as a recruit at Dänholm, off Stralsund, I noticed across the way in the other division my friend from Neustadt, who cheerfully bellowed across at me, 'Hi, Teddy, are you here too?' And from that moment on, in the Crew of '35, I became 'Teddy'. Only a tiny number knew my real first name. Such is life!

As I've said, I couldn't march; but riding was a different matter, for I had spent my childhood largely in the country. My father, whom I respected greatly, was a clever if somewhat conservative man. He had studied agriculture in Halle, and then emigrated to Samoa. In 1913 he returned to Germany,

Suhren with his brother and sister.

married my mother, and travelled back with her to the Pacific. A year later my brother was born, in Apia on Upolu, one of the main islands in German West Samoa. When the First World War broke out soon after that, my father packed his bags and sailed with my mother and the baby from American Pago-Pago to San Francisco. From New York they travelled out as Mr and Mrs Gasket and Junior on a Norwegian steamship to Bergen. My father's heavy growth of beard masked his student duelling-scars. He left his wife and child with her parents in Langenschwalbach [known today as Bad Schwalbach]. He himself went off to the Front as a Captain of Reserves with the 18th Leipzig Lancers. I don't think my mother ever got over having to leave the South Seas. In all her conversations about it one could always detect an almost unconscious longing for that lost Paradise.

I myself was born at my grandparents' home in Langenschwalbach on 16 April 1916. On my mother's side my forebears had been in the medical profession for many generations. My great-grandfather had been consultant gynaecologist to the Grand-Duchess of Hessen-Nassau. This lady was a daughter of Queen Victoria of England and she gave him an opening into just about all the ruling houses, including the Tsar's palace in St Petersburg. There he was even in charge of the medical team at the birth of the last Tsarevitch, who was a haemophiliac. My great-grandfather left the family his account book. Eugenie of France paid the most; on the other hand the Tsarina's page was completely empty. My great-grandfather had never closed the account, and the Tsarina had never paid him a rouble. This strange fact requires an explanation; both were quite clear about the fact that the money had been paid by the Tsarina but had never reached him; it was siphoned off *en route*.

However, the Tsarina, who was born Princess Alice von Hessen, nobly made up the deficiency, by presenting my Grandmother with an endless supply of sumptuous and valuable jewels. Right up to our generation our relatives had worn jewellery that originated from the last Tsarina; but in the course of twenty years of inflation all these valuables had been disposed of and were no more. We were all as poor as church mice.

After the First World War the English didn't allow the colonists of Samoa to return there. It is true that according to one clause of the Treaty of Versailles the emigrants dispossessed by the victorious powers were supposed to be compensated by the German government. But that never happened; we were left to fend for ourselves. My father became responsible for bigger and bigger areas; among other things he was Director of Agricultural Research in Saxony (*Direktor de Sächsichen Versüchsguter*), until it was disbanded. We became almost like brothers to his inspector, who was appropriately named 'Hobnail' – Hufnagel.

Despite the crisis in German agriculture, which became more and more noticeable over those twenty years, we had a happy childhood. We were able to play a lot of sport, and the nearest to hand was always riding. Even at the age of ten I had an hour's riding lesson every day from my father, so you could say I more or less grew up on horseback. Hence my love of

Suhren with his brother and father (*c*1941).

riding, which I have already mentioned, as well as my interest in sailing, which I pursued not just at the Hanseatic Yachting School but also at Spijkeroog, one of the Friesian Islands. That was at the Hermann Lietz School, which had a base there. That was a country boarding-school of the English type, at which along with academic lessons pupils were taught how to live in a community. These Hermann Lietz Schools still survive in the Federal Republic. Because of my father's changes of job it was simply one of a series of schools that I went through and whose communal life I enjoyed so much that learning didn't get much of a look-in. I spent too much time out on the water, and sailed with my older friend Alfred Haesler until my parents took me away. Though not particularly industrious, I survived, and in the fullness of time after Sorau, Haubinda and Spijkeroog I took my school-leaving exams at the state secondary school at Bautzen.

Even our choice of vocation was more or less dictated by circumstances. My brother was determined to be an engineer; I felt myself equally attracted to the sea and to medicine, following my mother's family. One career, however, my parents had never seriously considered: there was no money to be made from farming. The fact that our friend and neighbour Ihssen had once been a naval officer spoke for itself, and the desire to get out of my parents' pocket as quickly as possible settled it. My brother Gerd was lucky enough to be taken on in 1933 as a trainee Engineer Officer in the Reichsmarine, and I myself, the younger brother, was called up on 5 April 1935 to the 2nd Naval Division on the Baltic as a seaman-officer in training, in what was by then known as the Kriegsmarine.

My father, an old hand at these things, gave me a piece of advice for the road: 'You can't do anything, you don't know anything; to start with, make yourself out to be a dimwit – and be grateful that you are in a position to learn so many new things that are important for your life'. And that advice has never yet been proved wrong. At our house there was no conflict between generations. In all the free time that we enjoyed, I always listened to my father. That was also true as far as politics was concerned. National Socialism worried him. He got to realise very quickly that our new boss had surrounded himself with more or less questionable characters, and commented pointedly; 'When little people get overexcited with big ideas, the result is always a load of crap!' Later, when his fears were realised and the damage had been done, he once remarked; 'It was wrong that we conservatives held back in such a dignified way, instead of getting moving before it was too late and turning ourselves into an even stronger force to be reckoned with.'

That is all long past. Once embarked on our careers, inevitably, we only occasionally saw our parents again, and then at infrequent intervals. But my memories are of an untroubled and radiant youth, though eventually a shadow fell over that too. In 1945 my parents, who had had to wander so often and so far, found themselves in the Sudetenland. They didn't manage to escape and get away to safety. Perhaps they no longer wanted to. In Nu they were surrounded by Czechs. My father stole a march on them all; so that my mother and sister wouldn't fall into the hands of the raging mob, he put an end to their lives and committed suicide himself . . .

The German language possesses a number of sayings, which are so obvious that they are virtually platitudes; 'Once a use, ever a custom,' 'Years of learning are not the same as years of mastery', 'Everything is hard to begin with'. Today they are almost forgotten, but once they were on everyone's lips, even in the navy. But in spite of the exhausting nature of the basic training at Dänholm, we had a relatively pleasant and unstressful three months, which most of us regarded more as a sporting challenge. I got on well with our Korporal, Jodeit. Exchanges between us often relieved the tension; with his broad East Prussian accent they caused a good deal of merriment to the rest of the group. 'Seaman Suhren, three steps forward. Seaman Suhren, do you know what you are?' 'No, Herr Bootsmaat'. 'You are an ape. What are you?' 'I am an ape, Herr Bootsmaat.' 'Seaman Suhren, I've only one thing to say to you; these boots of yours are a disgrace not just to our platoon but to the entire German Navy.' 'Yes, Herr Bootsmaat . . .' 'What do you mean, "yes"? Are you trying to make fun of me?' 'No, Herr Bootsmaat'. Destiny had decreed that I be issued with a pair of high-boots (called 'diceboxes'), whose uppers had been sewn together with the rough side outward, and which it was therefore impossible to polish properly. Things generally ended with my having, as a punishment, to hop round the group like a penguin, holding my weapon in my outstretched arms with my knees bent. It got to the point that without any order I started to bend my knees and hop right at the start of the parade – which again incurred the disapproval of good old Jodeit. 'Seaman Suhren, are you taking the mickey again?' 'Yes sir, I mean no, Herr Bootsmaat.' Out of the kindness of his heart, he put an end to my misery one day by dragging me off to the clothing store and letting me change the 'diceboxes'. These little things are sent to try us!

It didn't stop at, 'Left, Right, Left . . .' and 'Squad, Quick March . . .'. Long route marches with packs followed, for which neither the navy in general nor I in particular managed to acquire a taste. We had no ambition to become infantrymen. They chased us one at a time carrying one of the old water-cooled machine guns through the sand dunes on the hills opposite. 'Attack, charge, charge . . .' Seaman Suhren couldn't help finding it funny; so he was made to give a solo performance after all the rest – there and back, with the machine gun: a duel, which made me sweat from every pore, and at which the rest were allowed to spectate, lying down, until Jodeit gave up and let me get my breath back. Years later he confided to me 'I've trained many recruits, and licked them all into shape – except one: and that was you!'

But I had a strong heart and a forgiving nature. I got on well with the other trainee officers. Similarly on the sail training ship *Gorch Fock*, on which we spent the next three months. I remember Bootsmaat Leisering, a thick-set fair-haired man, who we had no need to be afraid of; and there was Bootsmaat Kuddel Waterstrat, who used to take charge of us when we cleared the ropes away on deck, encouraging us with a cry of 'Move arrrrround, move arrrrround' – until we mimicked him, and continuously muttered to ourselves 'Move arrrrround,

The sail training ship *Niobe* sank in 1932 with the loss of 27 of its 49 cadets.

move arrrrround . . .' The man responsible for giving orders on deck was Oberbootsmann Kühn, a character well-known throughout the entire navy (he had previously survived the sinking of the *Niobe*), with his double-bass voice which was nurtured with copious quantities of alcoholic refreshment.

The *Gorch Fock* crossed the Baltic in summer, and we youngsters thought it was terrific. One of our favourite places was the safety-net under the jib-boom. Though it was forbidden, lying there in the jib-net in the darkness one was transported. We could watch the bow of the ship cutting through the phosphorescent water and dream of the wide world. During sailing manoeuvres each one of us – and there were round about 200 of us – had his allotted place. As one of the smallest, I stood right at the highest point, at the top of the main mast. Each mast did its best to be ready first. We were always trying to win the bet with the foremast.

Once we were anchored under the island of Fehmarn, not far from Stralsund, when a bit of a sea got going. A cutter, made fast alongside, threatened to break loose. I had the

The crew of a cutter struggles in a high sea.

anchor watch, so I got down there and secured it with another line. As I climbed back up the Jacob's ladder, a wave lifted the heavy cutter, and it crushed my leg against the side of the ship. The leg turned black and blue, and the considerable loss of blood drove me ashore into sick-bay. It looked as though I might have to break off my *Gorch Fock* training and be put back a crew. Indeed three weeks were spent in continuous exercises combined with physiotherapy, including massaging my leg and trying to straighten the knee by brute force, which was fiendishly painful. Eventually I overcame it by grim determination, and got through to Pillau to rejoin my crew on the sail training ship again, still weak at the knees, but nevertheless . . . My Korporal showed a bit of sympathy and let me down lightly. After some 'adjustments to the shrouds', I was soon up and running again.

At the end of our practical training on board, the *Gorch Fock* sailed to the Orkney Islands. In the night the wind got up, and as a result the topsails needed reefing. Under standing orders this was a job for under-officers only. But so as not to disturb their sleep, four of us 'babies' (that is, me and the other three on watch), went up top in the storm and the darkness. First the foremast, then the mainmast; between us we managed to get the flapping sails fastened down. In the end that brought the four of us a nice pat on the back.

Nevertheless, though I had thoroughly enjoyed my time on board the *Gorch Fock*, my memories of it are clouded by an event which had a lasting effect and dealt my good-humour a serious blow. At first we still wore tunics, whose tight collars chafed our necks, and made my tender skin red. The sun went out of its way to burn it, and made the edge of it dark, almost black. One day we were paraded in ordinary seaman's uniform for a 'cleanliness inspection'. I was glad of my open neck, but had forgotten about the dark stripes on it. The Divisional Officer cast only a fleeting glance at it, ordered me out front and by way of explanation told the grinning spectators that I was a dirty pig who couldn't wash himself properly. I was deeply hurt. My immediate reaction was that I had been unfairly treated: and still worse, my pride had been wounded. And by an officer, too. In search of help I made my way to Korporal Leisering. I suggested to him that we could go under the shower and try to wash away the mark. He answered, 'We don't need to do that; he knew perfectly well what it was.' I almost wept with anger, and continued, 'Herr Bootsmaat, from my point of view this public reprimand amounts to an insult to my honour.' Leisering stayed perfectly calm; 'Come on, Suhren, you just concentrate on doing your job here. Everything else is unimportant, whatever anyone else may say'. His matter-of-fact attitude impressed me, but my personal dignity had been wounded, and I made a resolution never thoughtlessly to hurt the feelings of anyone under my command in the future. It was regularly made clear to us that we were absolutely useless, so that we even took it in our stride when the Kommandant addressed us with the comment: 'If all you manage to achieve is to learn how to use toilet-paper properly, we shall all be highly delighted!'

The *Gorch Fock*, the sail training ship of the Kriegsmarine.

The romance of the sailing ship and the fascination of the sea-voyage *per se* allowed us to shut our eyes to this and similar events. In the end it wasn't so tough as it was made out to be. I realised in the meantime what the reality of the situation was. As trainee-officers we had to undergo 'Training-inspection', or 'Bildungsinspektion', known as the 'BI'. It was intended not only to train the next generation of sailors, but also to indoctrinate us. Instead of realising his own individual potential and using it accordingly, each young man had to be (to put it politely) 'standardised' and re-shaped. In addition, each of the officers of the BI was doing his utmost to be successful, so they outdid each other in their efforts to influence the new intake, or rather to break them in. Their group, their platoon, their company, their division had to be the best in every respect, so that they – and their career – might acquire some reflected glory from these achievements. Their arrogant but at the same time petty methods were all dedicated to one goal – to produce model soldiers; but what was the point of that?

Though I had a good relationship with the other trainee-officers I didn't manage to achieve the same thing with the officers of the BI. The incident on the *Gorch Fock* was only a early warning-sign. Apparently my mere appearance was tantamount to a provocation, especially since although I was one of the smallest I didn't pussy-foot around and didn't allow myself to be browbeaten. I was myself, and determined to stay so. Granted, as a trainee officer I was obliged to be a part of their team for the moment. But at the same time their team was not my team. That was just my opinion . . . No, I wouldn't want to expand on it. I felt that perhaps I was just the opposite of the bosses of the BI – at least it was always them who managed to get themselves the best jobs, and definitely not us, who were just a team of apprentices, unpolished or even outlandish as we were, and whose friendship it was to their advantage to resist. No, I swore silently to myself and promised myself never to turn into one of those ****s .

In September 1935 we became Seekadetten and received orders to report to the *Emden*, that was to take us on a nine-month foreign cruise to the Azores, Bermuda, the Caribbean, the West Coast of the USA and Hawaii, of which we didn't manage to see a lot, all things considered. The point of the training-cruise was to give us another complete course on the ship and its weapons; it felt however much the same. We cadets were put hard to work, harder than before, even harder than the crew. Young and fit though we were, we couldn't argue against it; we'd already learnt to make concessions to the Third Reich. Something else troubled us more. The ships' company was divided into two cadet watches and two watches of regular seamen, which were normally supposed to relieve each other in rotation. But, as they explained patiently to us, they were keen that we should be able to devote more time to training, so the regular crew took turns on watch at sea, and we sea-cadets had to stand anchor-watch in port instead. That was not

The *Emden* returns from a goodwill cruise before the outbreak of war.

entirely fair, and stood the whole point of the foreign cruise completely on its head. It should have been the trainee officers who had priority in getting a look at foreign ports, lands and peoples, to complement their academic knowledge, as a means of broadening their view of the world. Later there would be hardly any opportunity. By contrast, on the merchant ships, seaman-officers' duties were limited almost without exception to home and neighbouring waters. In our case the foreign cruise was in fact principally for the benefit of the regular crew. They could do what we couldn't. In harbour we cadets could only try to swap watches and have a go at trying to get shore-leave with the rest of the official shore-party. For instance in dreamily beautiful Hawaii, where we spent twelve days, I actually managed to get ashore three times for a few hours – and that was my experience of 'foreign ports, countries and people'!

I do remember, however, that I managed to make a date with a young lady in La Guaira, the outer harbour of Caracas, Venezuela. It was on a Sunday. But on this particular Sunday my distinguished training-officer – nay, exceptionally distinguished – decided to call a locker-inspection. It was a particularly good method of education, a means both of occupying his time for him and of keeping us from going off the rails; for in the meantime a swell had got up, and there were no more boats ashore, and my lovely girl-friend had to wait ashore in her Packard in vain. That was Sunday gone for a burton.

In the locks of the Panama Canal, I was bowman, keen as ever, with the job of making the lines fast. It was about Christmas time, pretty hot and humid as far as we were concerned; the sweat ran off us in streams. And just as we were toiling away with the tow-lines at the E-lock, our third training officer, scarcely any older than us, threw his hands up dramatically. How lucky we were to be seeing so much of the world at our age. I lost patience with him and burst out, 'OK, let's swap places then . . .'. The Leutnant felt insulted. He made his way to the senior officer, complaining that it was quite unheard of and positively mutinous, and I should be put on report and disciplinary action taken. The senior officer, who knew that I had a tendency to be outspoken, laughed up his sleeve and managed to dissuade him from it. So it was left at that. But the Leutnant was also signals officer, and managed to even the score with me. His hobbyhorse was the thick naval code-book, with hundreds of phrases in it which he made us learn by heart; and a painful task it was too. I had other ideas, and was more interested in morse and semaphore. If I could master that (and I was determined to do so) I would not have to rely later on being kept informed by signals personnel, but be in a position of being able to control all messages myself. So, learn the signal-book by hand, no! But the training officer kept testing me on this too. I said, 'Herr Leutnant, can't we give it a miss? The code-book is only like a telephone book; you've just got to open it up to check whether you've got the right number or not, surely?' In the end it was all I could do, despite my outstanding ability in matters of signalling, not to fail the exam.

On the next leg of the voyage they handled us cadets rather more liberally, and let us go ashore more often. Especially in Portland, Oregon, the hospitable Americans offered us every facility. Among other things I remember a dance with teenagers at which my crewmate Hein Uphoff got acquainted with 'Baby'. He took a delight in rolling her name around his tongue with great relish. Unfortunately Baby had a girl-friend with her, and Hein wanted to off-load her somehow. So he came to me and said, 'Teddy, can't you take Baby's girl-friend off my hands for me?' I took a look at her girl-friend and shook my head: 'Hein, she's not my type, you can't ask me to do that, no way. Surely you can see that for yourself, if you think about it.' Hein became angry, and reacted strongly. 'Come on, are you my friend or not?' I answered, 'There's no need for you to have go at me like that, thank you.' And what was the end result? I allowed myself to be talked round, but said right away to Baby, 'If you come again tomorrow with the same girl-friend, and don't bring a different one with you that I fancy, then it's all over with Hein. Be absolutely clear about that.'

The next day Baby brought a young American girl with her called Dolores. Now I could let the name 'Dolores' roll around my tongue, and all in all it worked out tremendously well. When it was time for us to leave port, I was presented with a lovely photo as a leaving-present. I kept it for a long time afterwards, and later when I was married my wife actually hung it on the wall in our house; the photo of a sweet little teenager with the dedication, in English, 'To my dearest Teddy, from Dolores'.

When our training ship arrived at Baltimore/Maryland, we cadets caught the train to New York in order to take home some impressions of the metropolis. We spent the night on a passenger-steamer of the Hamburg-America Line at the HAPAG pier in Manhattan. In the organised programme there was a gap of three hours which we decided to fill in by having a stroll around. It was 1936, and there was some concern that opponents of the Hitler regime might possibly give us some trouble on the streets, so we did our best not to look like typical Nazi stereotypes. The cadet officer sent us off, warning us to go out in groups of two or better still of three or four, and to be back on time. But there didn't seem to be a problem. Downtown we weren't molested at all, never mind attacked. If anything people were just curious, and stared at us to see if we were wearing any Nazi emblems – swastikas and so on. We behaved ourselves quite normally, as young cadets, and there was no trouble. Only on one occasion did a black man come up to us and address us; 'Hello, what's the German Kaiser doing? Is he in Holland, chop plenty wood?' I remembered learning from my parents some of the Pidgin-English which they used to speak in the South Seas, which they always talked so enthusiastically about. So I retorted in a similar patois: 'Me no sabby too muchee . . .'. The black man became angry; 'You bloody damn German, you'll see the niggers in the next war';

and he disappeared back into the crowd. That was the only untoward incident we experienced in Manhattan.

My brother, two years older than me, and belonging to the Crew of '33, was trained on the other training ship, the *Karlsruhe*. Their journey in fact took them to Samoa, and so my brother was fortunate enough to get to know these distant islands in the Pacific, on which he had first glimpsed the light of day in 1914. And there the surprise of his life was waiting for him. As he was dancing with a young girl, she looked him up and down and then announced that there was on the island a young man, pretty much the same age as him, who looked extraordinarily like him. My brother, Gerd Suhren, said, becoming curious, 'What's his name, then?' The answer came, incredibly, 'His name is John Suhren'!

How about that! So we came to discover by chance something about our cousin in Samoa. It was all to do with the son of my late godfather and uncle Reinhard Suhren, who died in 1919, and his Samoan wife. This man, our cousin, had produced offspring, and one of his other sons (also called Reinhard Suhren), as we discovered had managed in the third generation to produce ten children – probably due to the seductive effects of the climate and the beauty of the women. So, as you can see, both as a German colony and as a protectorate of New Zealand, Samoa is still in hands of the Suhrens!

3

Mürwik – A disastrous Rosenmontag – 'I intend to resign' – Belated revenge

THE NAVAL ACADEMY AT MÜRWIK is a red-brick building and looks like a mock-Gothic castle from the time of the Kaiser. From the steep bank of the Flensburg estuary its imposing facade looks straight out over the wide expanse of water into the distance; 'Full steam ahead!' However, the view doesn't extend as far as all that. After just a few kilometres the view is broken by the green hills of Denmark.

Gone were the Hula-Hula songs of Hawaii; we had to make do with a chorus in the canteen. For after the *Gorch Fock*, and the foreign cruise, we, that is, the Crew of '35, were posted here to the place where previous generations of up-and-coming naval officers had pursued their academic studies; maths, navigation, maritime law, tactics, ship building, weaponry, languages and a few more subjects too. Externally we had undergone a change in appearance. The Kiel sailor's uniform, with the flap behind the neck, called a 'sailor-suit', was a thing of the past. Now we wore a day-shirt and a tie, a jacket with a narrow silver shoulder-tab, and a peaked cap, white from May till September, and blue in the winter months, as appropriate. In addition, the sailor's dagger, of course without a sword-belt. We had become midshipmen. A midshipman without a sword-belt was the same rank as an under-officer, and had no authority; on the contrary we had a lot to learn.

The Crew of '35 comprised over 400 young people from all walks of life. We were divided up into four companies, then

The Naval Training College at Flensburg-Mürwik.

into platoons, and then into smaller groups – classes, for example; and in the Naval Academy we were kept pretty busy. I can't recall too many details of it, but nevertheless a few essential facts that they dished up to us stick in the mind. For instance; 'From the moment when the German Kaiser intervened in ship-building in 1915 it went rapidly downhill'; and, 'I have observed that only the Good, the Brave and the Obedient get on in the Navy'. That last one reminds me of the 'Ten Commandments of the German Soldier', which came out at that time, and which hung in every recruit's room; it represented a example for us to follow, 'self-confident yet unassuming, fearless and loyal'.

Our teacher in the School of Gunnery, a subject on which I was particularly keen, was 'Kanon-Willi'. He had been a gunnery officer at the Battle of Skagerrak [Jutland], and told vivid stories about it, in particular how in the general excitement he had forgotten to switch the shells over from percussion fuses to armour-piercing, which considerably reduced their penetrating power. At this point a tremble came into his

Sander, Ey, Uphoff, Brandi, Suhren, and Schütze at Mürwik 1937.

voice, because of the opportunity they had missed to destroy another wicked British battleship. Despite their former professional enmity, 'Kanon-Willi' had married an English girl. As a result of this, at the outbreak of the war he found himself in a tragic situation of conflicting loyalties. He condemned the continuing hostilities, and continuously bemoaned his misfortune. Sadly he did it once too often, and was suddenly given the chop.

Just a word on our grading for 'Service aptitude' at the Academy. Marks went from 1 to 9, 9 being the ideal. Only marks above 5 were worth anything; if one scored less than that it was impossible for one to pass the Seaman Officers' final exam. Even a score of 5 counted as OK, and didn't require any great effort from us. Of course it was only necessary for one of the BI officers to remark, 'You'll struggle to score 3 with me . . .'. In each individual subject there were separate marks awarded, and when nine months were up these went to make up your 'Service aptitude' mark; that was how the overall result was calculated. The final mark determined your future progress in the navy and was therefore extremely important; for if you achieved a high overall score, you lay in the upper part of the year's mark-order. This method might have seemed at first glance to be objective, and to provide a reliable method of assessing the up-and-coming naval officers. Unfortunately, like all marking procedures of this sort it could be distorted by the personal preferences and dislikes of individual superior officers; this led to questionable results, and succeeded in giving a false picture. If your face didn't suit the instructors, you suffered for it – which meant that in the final result the navy itself was worse off. As for me, I had a relatively high score of 7.5 and nothing to fear. Until Rosenmontag, the day before Shrove Tuesday, arrived . . .

Since we had Rhinelanders among us, who at about twenty years old were hardly toddlers, it was felt necessary to celebrate the [Catholic] Carnival Festival with due jollity even though we were in the [Protestant] North of Germany. All the midshipmen were given leave until 06.00, except for our division; our famous divisional-officer wanted to make a name for himself by exceptional devotion to duty, so he cut our leave by an hour and fixed our time of reporting back at 05.00. I had joined a different and more cheerful group of mates and went off with them to Flensburg. The maidens were only too happy to allow themselves to be swept onto the dance-floor by us midshipmen. Beer, wine and champagne flowed freely (which is why it's so great on the Rhine!) and the time flew by. I had completely forgotten that my mates were allowed to stay out longer than I was. I happened to glance at the clock, and it was just before 5 o'clock. Panic!

I rushed out of the bar, looked in vain for a taxi, and started the long trek back to Mürwik. On the way the first tram overtook me, and I managed to jump on. But it was already getting late, and it was a few minutes past five in the morning when I passed through the gates of the Naval Academy. There stood a keen officer of my company, his watch in his hand. 'Where have you been, then?' My answer was clear and simple – 'At Carnival'. His bitter-sweet retort was, 'Fine – on report tomorrow with the Head of Company for overstaying leave.'

My cheerful frame of mind – after all, Carnival and Rosenmontag come but once a year – gave way to deep depression. As far as I was concerned it turned into Ash Wednesday. In a few weeks we were to sit the Seaman Officers' exam, and the consequences could not be overlooked. In order to save my skin I tried to swing it with the officer of the watch and the signing-out book. That counted against me even more when I stood in front of the Company Boss the next morning, a worried little twenty-year-old. It was clear that my mere appearance already had the same effect on many people as the proverbial red rag to a bull. You can imagine with what dislike, indeed almost hatred, the Korvettenkapitän regarded me. My mates must have been able to overhear the growing list of crimes of which I was supposed to be guilty. In short, I was the worst individual one could possibly imagine. I broke out in a sweat, and shook all over. In the end, I just switched off, since everything in me denied these accusations. And the whole time my divisional-officer stood near me saying nothing; he, who had rated me so highly, heard all these accusations against one of his midshipmen – who trusted him – and never said a word to contradict it. He didn't even put in a good word for me when the company boss finally gave me a sentence of five days confined to barracks. This infuriated me even more. When I'd been given my five-day sentence, I went up to him and snarled, 'Half of that should properly be yours, Herr Kapitänleutnant'. And I was off before the two of them could get over the shock.

But the worst was yet to come. My 'service aptitude' mark was reduced from 7.5 to 4, and all my fine divisional-officer had to say was, 'If you really try hard, we'll see whether we can give you a 5, and with the 5 you'll still be able to pass the officer's exam. ' I had five days to ponder it in. When I reported back again afterwards, furious and unbowed, he seemed somehow disappointed; 'Your detention doesn't seem to have much effect on your attitude,' he commented pointedly. This time I didn't beat about the bush. 'Herr Kapitänleutnant,' I said, 'I agree absolutely that punctuality is necessary. But why was our company given leave till 5 o'clock and all the others till 6? It's deliberate victimisation. Are we worse than all the others? And as for me' – and here my hackles rose – 'I was previously one of the best in your group with a mark of 7.5, and on account of a mere trifle of a few minutes at Carnival time that's been reduced to 4; now is that fair? How can you justify that? I didn't spend all that time becoming a competent recruit, serving on the *Gorch Fock* and the *Emden*, just to be put back to square one in my career in the navy on account of a mere triviality. I cannot accept that.'

The problem was not specifically the confinement, a sentence that one just sits out on one's backside, but the marks. The 'service mark' was reduced, and that automatically had the effect of reducing all one's individual marks. In short, despite my having been one of the best of the crew, I was about to plummet just about to the bottom; in fact I was virtually reduced to the ranks. And that being the case, one was, to put it bluntly, scarcely worth marrying in naval circles. One moment spent in the ranks was enough for a prospective father-in-law to raise both hands in the air; 'Just don't have him, girl, in heaven's name, no good will come of him . . .'. And that's the long and the short of it. It goes without saying that a marriage within naval circles was then considered all-important.

I managed to get through the naval officers' exam. As one of the best in the naval academy, they couldn't very well fail me, as they would really loved to have done. But my record, complete with all the consequent crap from the BI bosses attached to it, accompanied me to the 1st Destroyer Division, where I finally ended up on the *Max Schultz* for further practical training. I came across my divisional-officer from the Naval Academy later in the war, by the way. By then I was highly decorated, and his equal in rank. He was on his way home with his submarine suffering from belly-ache and I took four of his torpedoes off him. More of that later.

The 1st Destroyer Division lay in Swindemunde, and consisted of four ships; *Leberecht Maas*, *Max Schultz*, *Richard Beitzen* and *Georg Thiele*. The Captain of my destroyer, the *Max Schultz*, had previously been Kadettenofficer on the cruiser *Karlsruhe*, and treated us midshipmen in exactly the same way. I was in his bad books right from the start, and he was just waiting for the opportunity to show it to me. It soon came. I was responsible for the destroyer's boats, that is, the tender and the pinnace. Along with that I was also responsible for the use of the boats which travelled across from the dock in Ostswine to Swinemünde where the married quarters were. That was a good distance away, right across the Swine. On this particular day the Obersteuermann was officer of the watch. And one PO after another wanted exclusive use of the pinnace, so I suggested to the Obersteuermann, 'Couldn't we combine all these mates of yours together? Then the boat would only need to make one journey instead of burning up five times the amount of fuel?' All I'd done was to make a suggestion, but of course he had nothing more urgent to do than to tell the commander that I'd refused to obey his orders. The commander understood nothing about navigation and so had got into the habit of accepting what the navigation-officer told him; so when he set eyes on me after parade I knew I was for it again. I couldn't get a word in edgewise. And having once got started, not to put too fine a point on it he gave me a dog's life on the cruise over the next month.

On another occasion we went to sea for target practice – 'Clang-disc shooting'. The 'Clang-disc' was a buoy with a metal plate on it. It was used for target-practice by guns which had a rifle mounted alongside the muzzle. This was a way of saving shells but at the same time gave us practice in aiming the gun; with each hit you got a 'clang' – hence the name. As 'boss of the boats' I sat in the launch which pulled the target. The

The *Leberecht Maas*, sister-ship of the *Max Schultz*, from the 1st Destroyer Division then based at Swinemünde.

destroyer *Richard Beitzen* was last to shoot before it was our turn to have a go. It took off at high speed, smoke pouring from its funnels. In the wake it threw up, the 'clang-target' capsized. It was just before dusk, and unless I could manage to get it upright again right away, we wouldn't get a go at it ourselves and the day would be lost. I turned round and with a mate on the helm drove as quickly as I could to where the buoy had capsized; but at the precise moment that I tried to right the target with a boat-hook, my mate put the engine into reverse, as I had specifically told him not to do. At once the tow-line got tangled round the propeller, and the boat was immobilised. What now? It was November, and pretty cold. So as not to make a bad situation worse, I dived in three times in full uniform to try to free the propeller. No good – another boat had to put out to tow us back along with the target. We never did get another go at shooting. On board in due course I copped it from the Captain. I must be the most stupid bird-brain in the world – and certainly the worst on the base. There was nothing left for me to do but agree with him with the usual

'Jawohl, jawohl.' I hadn't exactly enjoyed the experience myself. While I was putting on some dry clothes, the First Officer sent for me. Ah dear God, him as well! But things turned out quite differently from what I had expected. Kapitänleutnant von Bechtolsheim-Mauchenheim invited me into his cabin. 'Sit down, Midshipman Suhren. I watched the whole thing through my binoculars. Your diving in impressed me. Getting a rope round the prop is something that can happen to anyone. However, it hasn't done anything for the reputation you enjoy with the Captain' – and here he gave me a meaningful look. 'But chin up! And just to warm you up a bit, what about a stiff grog?' I must say, I was as grateful and touched as a much-beaten dog that someone finally pats. It had done me a bit of good after all! Now I had at least one person on my side, and moreover the Number One. And I was able to cash in on it as well; for misfortune quickly struck again. It was during a night shooting exercise with the Division. All four destroyers were shooting with the 12.7cm gun at a target-ship – I think it was the old *Hanover*. This time we fired with shells which went off with a proper detonation, and they made a pretty good bang. We went for it hell for leather. The plating of the worn-out ship glowed from the sheer number of hits on it. We were the third destroyer, and so close to it that our searchlight directed onto the target only made a tiny circle of light. The searchlight was operated by my crew-mate Kolbe, the son of Admiral Kolbe, the erstwhile boss of the instructor corps. I stood behind the rangefinder on the bridge wing; no one could see me. The *Hanover*, glowing from all the direct hits, was perfectly visible even without the feeble searchlight. I stood there, suspecting nothing amiss, and was suddenly loudly reprimanded. 'Make way for the search-light officer!' When all was said and done, I wasn't in the way. 'Kolbe', I retorted, 'what's up with you? You're talking out of your back-side. Watch your gob!' But then it happened again; 'Suhren, get out of the light!' Inevitably the commander overheard it too, and he soon started as well; 'Suhren, get out of the light,

The Kriegsmarine target ship *Hessen*.

what's the big idea?' and so on. So eventually I climbed one deck higher, where I would be out of harm's way.

However there were a number of guests on board attending the target-practice, and Kolbe had kept trying to bring it to their attention that he was the son of Admiral Kolbe. I thought I could give him a helping hand, so I bent over the rails from the artillery control deck, and said in a clear drawl – 'Now then, Midshipman Kolbe, can you see anything now?' 'Ah, dear God, why don't you shut up?' came the inevitable reply. Then a runner from the Old Man came up out of breath; 'The Midshipman is requested to report to the commander below decks.' I went. 'Midshipman reporting, sir!' The commander was even smaller than me, and stood over me on a sort of high wooden decking, almost speechless with fury. 'You shameless midshipman, who do you think you're talking to, what do you think you're doing, where are you . . .?' The lecture ended as usual with the bellow – 'On report in the morning!'

An iron silence surrounded me instantly. I was sent to Coventry; I had the plague. The officers, Leutnant, Oberleutnant, the whole of the BI training team, would no longer sit at the same table as me. As far as they were concerned

I was the Invisible Man. My only ally was the First Officer. He came up to me; 'Suhren, tell me what's up.' He almost died laughing. I replied, sadly, that I hadn't meant any harm by it, and was just trying to draw the guests' attention to Fähnrich Kolbe. 'Aha – do you know what the commander said to me? "He'd better watch out, that Suhren; he's made a monkey out of me, and in front of everyone too".' 'But Herr Kapitänleutnant', I replied,' I wouldn't dare to do that. I really didn't do that, I swear it.' Von Bechtolsheim sighed; 'Well, we'd better wait for the Report in the morning. I'll be there though,' he added to cheer me up.

The Report began badly enough; in fact it got going full blast straight away. The Old Man shouted at me, 'If I didn't happen to know your brother, who is a distinguished officer, you'd be out of the Navy today!' That was pretty strong stuff. Then the First Officer chipped in; his smile had left him. 'Herr Kapitän', he said firmly, 'I'd like to say a good word for Teddy. He didn't intend his remark to be any reflection on yourself; he just wanted our guests to be aware of the son of Admiral Kolbe'. Well, as soon as he heard the word Admiral the commander immediately calmed down. He asked for an account of the whole thing, but punished me in the end with six weeks loss of leave. That wasn't so terrible, but it did mess up my nice weekends. I was accustomed to spending the weekends with my friend Hufnagel, who had served under my father in Saxony as an inspector. He was now head of the state horse farm at Ferdinandshof, in the region of Stettin. I was able to ride with him to my heart's content or travel through the woods in a carriage, and forget all my troubles. But because of this, for the moment it had to be cancelled.

Despite all, I got over the incident, found in the First Officer an understanding superior, and tried my best. Nevertheless, I was no longer content with my life. The continuous misunderstandings and slights had had their effect. They made me dispirited and lacklustre. I didn't cause any particular problems again; but I still couldn't shake off the reference from the

Naval Academy that had followed me. I was not destined to be a model-soldier of any consequence. And however much effort I made, the commandant still disliked me. In the end everything had gone wrong.

My mate whom I have already mentioned above was right when he summed up the situation in broad Berlin dialect; 'Midshipman, I tell you, once you've got yourself well and truly in the shit, nothing can help you; you'll always be in the shit. However hard you try, even if you come out with top marks, no one notices any more. And at the end of the day the Old Man is determined to shit on you too, for treading his corns too hard into the deck.'

It got to Christmas. During the holidays our promotion to Oberfähnrich was announced with effect from 1 January 1938. But this didn't help me much any more. I was no longer enjoying life. At home I met my brother, who was already a Leutnant, and told him, very upset, 'Gerd, I intend to resign from the navy . . .'. My brother was shocked. 'My God, you can't do that, think of the shame you'd bring on our parents. You've got to find some way of surviving.' I determined to, despite all. It was simply that I couldn't see any future for me in the Navy any more. The gentlemen of the BI, the hardliners, had finished me off. Indeed my commander at that time, who never lost an opportunity to grind me underfoot, had finished me off to such an extent that no one wanted to have any more to do with me. 'Well then', my brother interjected, 'you must change the way you behave towards your present commander'. I looked at him uncomprehendingly. 'And how should I behave differently towards him? Do what I may, it doesn't cut any ice with him.' My brother dug out a postcard. 'Now, watch this! We're going to write to your commander right away. He was my cadet-officer too: "Esteemed Captain, I am delighted to be able to spend Christmas with my brother Teddy at our parents' house. My brother Teddy speaks so enthusiastically of the Navy, and how much he is enjoying it on the *Max Schultz* . . .'. 'At this point I cried out, 'I can't and I won't sign that!' My brother was unruffled. 'You sign it, send some nice New Year greetings below, and shut up.' 'I can't add how much I enjoy it on his destroyer. That's out of the question'. 'Then just add a PS below', said my brother firmly. 'Write underneath – "Happy New Year to you and your most respected wife Frau Gemahlin". That's all, you don't need to write any more'. In the end I allowed myself to be talked into signing it.

The effect was staggering. As soon as I'd arrived back from holiday, and even while I was still getting changed, up came the runner with the K-armband whom I knew so well by now. 'Oberfähnrich Suhren to report to the commanding-officer!' 'Hey, Teddy, you've only just got on board. What have you done this time?' 'I haven't done anything – I don't think . . .' I thought, I don't believe this. The commander came smiling up to me and gave me a friendly greeting. 'My dear Suhren, may I return your New Year's Greeting most heartily, and congratulate you on your promotion? I had no idea that you were enjoying it so much in the Navy,' – and so, and so forth. In response to an enquiry from my mate Jurgen Sander, who had assumed the worst, I explained casually, 'I don't know what you mean. He just wished me a Happy New Year and thanked me for my greeting. Did you write him a card?' 'No, I didn't think of it, actually'. 'Well, ' I replied, 'that's where you went wrong. You won't be able to make up for it that easily; New Year only happens once a year.' Straight away things improved. Also, I didn't have much longer to do on board. On 1 April I became a Leutnant, and immediately transferred to the submarine service. Whatever had died in me revived right away in the submarine service.

When we met again years later, there was a postscript. My former commander had in the meantime become Konteradmiral and Head of Officer Appointments. When he saw me with some others he gave a start of surprise and came over to greet me right away; 'My dear Suhren, how good it is to see you again. What fun we had together on the *Max Schultz*, what?' But by then I was no longer a little midshipman, but a Korvettenkapitän, having had the benefit of accelerated promotion; I was decorated with swords to my Iron Cross and could risk saying what I thought. So I looked full at him and said to him in the silence which had suddenly fallen, drawling clearly, like that time on the destroyer, 'A "fun" time? For you possibly, Herr Admiral; for me it was the crappiest time of my entire life.' There was an embarrassed silence around us. Everything suddenly stopped dead. His smile froze on his face. He went as white as a sheet, didn't say another word and made himself scarce. And that should have been the end of the story. But it wasn't. At the time I'm referring to, he was in charge of officer personnel. And he took his revenge on me in return by putting a line through my promotion to Captain, which would normally have fallen due automatically. Before the situation could be put right, the war had come to an end.

4

Another world – 1WO in the Atlantic – War: 'Stop at once!' – 'Take heart, take heart'

WHEN ONE THINKS OF SUBMARINES, one inevitably thinks of Karl Dönitz, who commanded the German submarine service during the Second World War. When I got to know him, first as Kapitän zur See and then as Kommodore, he was 'Führer der U-boote' (FdU). I served in the 7th Submarine Flotilla, the 'Wegener', and was watch officer on *U-48* under Kapitänleutnant Herbert Schultze. My acquaintance with the FdU got off to a rather unpromising start. That too was over a matter of shooting. In the summer of 1938 the flotilla was conducting gunnery practice, and was firing with the 8.8cm gun at a target ship anchored in the distance. We on *U-48* waited sixth in line for our attempt. The boats before us fired away with all guns blazing – literally! Dönitz was there as spectator, and landed eventually rather crossly on *U-48*, a thin man in his late forties. The commander welcomed him on board. I was on the bridge, and reported to him as artillery officer, whereupon he remarked; 'Are your thumbs broken?' I glanced down, and saw that I had my thumbs spread out wide like a half-moon inside the thick protective leather gloves. 'No, Herr Kommodore!' 'Then get on with the job!'

Damn – a really promising start! Later I was all set to go on *U-48*, the old thunder-box. It was a matter of planning a difficult approach while firing, with the target ship making some turns to try to avoid the pursuing attackers. It was important to keep a close eye on it as it twisted and turned so as to get a

Karl Dönitz, commander of the German U-boat force throughout the Second World War (at Angers/Chateau Pignerolles).

sideways approach to it. At the instant of its turning, when it offered a good target for a few moments, I got it perfectly lined up, and called to the gun crew, 'Five rounds rapid fire! Quick, hurry!' The number 1 of the gun crew, who was supposed to pull the trigger, looked blankly at me instead of shooting. In a surge of impatience I leapt onto the gun-platform and shouted, 'Come on, man, get out of the bloody way!' In fact, we got four direct hits, and the head of the Flotilla reported proudly, 'First rate shooting, Herr Kommodore.' Dönitz was not happy about it; 'I'm not impressed. Tell the gunnery officer to report to me.' When I stood in front of him – yet again – he started on a dressing-down right away. 'I don't want to hear any more of this sort of language.' I was ordered not to employ expressions of my own, but to use, if you please, the proper naval terminology that had been found perfectly adequate for decades. 'Jawohl, jawohl'; there wasn't any more for me to say. I must have presented a very sorry sight, for the Kommandant 'Vati' Schultze commented afterwards to me,

'What are you worried for? It doesn't mean much. Dönitz has always had a bad temper. On the other hand, you shot well, and that's what matters.'

My good score was no fluke. As a result of my good eyesight I was a gifted gunner. Already during gunnery training my visual ability to make good spatial judgements had made for success. When we were midshipmen we had to shoot at a towed target in the finals of the shooting competition. I found it easy to spot whether the shots fell just short of the target or beyond it, and always managed to get the third shot on target, that is, right in the bullseye. After that all we had to do was adjust the distance as we approached. I was amazed how well it all worked, and was delighted when the boss of the Academy said, 'I'd like to know the name of that man; I have never seen a midshipman shoot so well.'

We were always supposed to explain our shooting at a 'post-mortem' in front of everyone, according to a complicated established procedure. Now in artillery shooting there is a standard method which one is supposed to keep to. However, because of my good eyesight I found that I could short-cut this performance, and was able to rely on my own judgement to get on target more quickly; but I tended to forget that not everyone had my spatial perception, and that the shooting procedure was cooked up for a normal eye, with the result that they found the target more slowly but with more certainty. To cut a long story short, at the post-mortem I let fall a distinctly unacceptable remark about the longwinded 'proper procedure', that reduced the whole class to laughter. As a result the commander of the Academy tore me off a strip in no uncertain way in front of everyone. He would have thought . . . I ought to be . . . in all truth what should happen to me . . . And taking all things into consideration I 'lacked the proper maturity to become a gunnery officer'. So that was how I managed to cross swords with him too.

My transfer to the submarine service came about without any action on my part. I had frequently voiced the opinion that

I could see myself in that kind of a role, but it fell on deaf ears. On the contrary, my superiors in the BI would dearly have liked to give me a command with the land-forces and make me creep about in the sand. However, I got on remarkably well with the FdU (and later BdU), who didn't hold our first meeting against me. Not being one to rely on his first impressions, Dönitz was not prone to proceeding on the basis of a quick glimpse of a man. On the contrary, he kept a close eye on his people, and revised his opinion if he found it to be incorrect. As a way of double-checking, he then took his time in acting. I believe I was actually given accelerated promotion after my wretched training-record had been shown to be irrelevant. Perhaps it helped that I was always open and honest with him, not concealing what I was trying to say, and didn't try to make anything seem either better or worse than it was. He never took my opinions and lines of argument amiss, though they were often very negative; on the contrary he valued them highly.

With my transfer to the submarine service, suddenly a whole new world opened up for me. It wasn't so much the technical details of weapons, which we made a start on with a special course on torpedoes at Mürwik. The torpedo is of course the unique weapon of the submarine. There were more types that were developed later; but our standard 'eel' was 7m [23ft] long, had a diameter of 53cm [21in], weighed one and a half tons, and carried in its replaceable warhead an explosive charge weighing 300kg [662lbs], which detonated on contact. Driven by an electric motor and propellers, it travelled towards the target at a depth that was previously set. Though they didn't look like it, these greasy, glistening, steel cigars were capable of travelling in exceptional circumstances as far as 14km. Normally, in near and rapid shooting, one needed to be much closer for the attack. Every torpedo that missed its target eventually sank.

Nor was it a question of the much-quoted 'Deep Sea World'. We got acquainted here with the smallest type of submarine,

One of the tiny 'canoes' from the training flotilla at Neustadt.

the so-called 'canoes' of only 250 tons, belonging to the training flotilla based at Neustadt. Our training here included the 'diving tank', in which we practised getting out of a sunken submarine wearing a diving-escape outfit, a life-jacket filled with oxygen. In calm waters it had already proved successful, especially in the case of *U-18* after its collision in Lübeck bay.

One wouldn't stand much chance of escaping in the Atlantic, however, with its greater depth of water.

No: it was the fact that in this other world I found waiting for me a whole set of better moral values, such as understanding, comradeship, human sympathy and even warmth. I had been accustomed to being pushed around, and had quite thought that all these virtues were already a thing of the past; but now I came back to life, and felt myself more at home in the navy by the day. No-one could have suspected that all this was like a loan that would have to be repaid in a few years time as a result of the sheer number of casualties, which no one could have predicted.

No longer did they treat us like ignoramuses. They saw in us the submarine officers of the future. Here it was not a matter of being under command, and being ordered around. Suggestions were made in a reasonable manner as to what we should learn and what we should avoid. Also, on board the training-boat an informal relationship prevailed with the resident officers, as it would also between Kommandant and LI (Chief Engineer). Off-duty we acquired privileges which we had previously been denied. With four friends I bought a used Opel, christened it 'Emma', and with it terrorised the coast road up as far as Timmendorf Beach and Travemünde, where the girls would exclaim joyfully, 'Emma's back again!' Once we had a puncture. A Kommandant passed and asked us, 'What's up then?' Then he gave us his spare tyre. We were quite unaccustomed to this kind of gesture. It seemed as though we hadn't quite woken up yet, as we started out on our service career! Nevertheless no-one gave us a hard time; everything went brilliantly. One thing we felt, with all – indeed because of all – this freedom; we must make every effort here, and work to earn the goodwill, hopefully even the confidence, of our superior officers. Basically we all became friends with each other. During the watch-officers' course I was posted to *U-1*, and following that, right up to the outbreak of the Second World War, I was put with LI Stahmer, who instructed us in practical submarine theory.

The Weddingen Flotilla, named after one of the most distinguished U-boat commanders of the First World War.

We were still very young. The submarine service was just building up, and was still very small. Everyone knew everyone else. The flotillas, named after distinguished commanders of the First World War (Weddingen, Saltwedel, etc) were periodically re-divided in order to establish new flotillas. The consequence was that eventually all the flotillas were fragmented. The FdU, Dönitz, had his staff quarters in Sengwarden, near Wilhelmshaven. The No 2 FdU, then Kapitän and later Admiral von Friedeburg, was stationed on the accommodation vessel at Kiel. His personal responsibility was for supply: in short, he was the vital quartermaster of the submarine service.

After all the courses had come to an end, I was posted to the 7th U-Flotilla, the 'Wegener', and there assigned to *U-48*. However, *U-48* was still under construction, though shortly to be commissioned. So in view of the shortage of officers I was lent out to other boats in the meantime, which just then were being required to spend more weeks practising in the Atlantic, and which were obliged to have two watch officers on board. I had three tours of duty as watch officer, on various boats in the Atlantic: *U-51* with Heinicke, *U-46* with Sohler, and *U-47* with Prien. I fired a lot of torpedoes at distant boats, and learnt everything I could. I found out from experience how individual commanders ran their boats – and also discovered how not to do it! Scarcely anyone in the submarine service had a better weapons- and watch-officer training.

After the last Atlantic trip, on which Engelbert Endrass was 1WO, I was switched to *U-48*, which had been completed in the meantime – and, despite all, as 1WO, which amounted to an internal promotion. Those responsible felt it appropriate because of my experience and my reputation. I was also confident in my own abilities in a variety of ways. On one occasion I brought a boat back through the English Channel. The 1WO was below, and I didn't want to send for him. Why should I, if I was confident I could do the job myself? But today, I have to admit that it was only the frantic morse signals from the merchant vessels – 'Alter course to port!' which prevented me from putting the boat on a sandbank under the French coast! Of course I was able to bring all my experience to bear for the benefit of *U-48*, especially on the occasion when the Kommandant, Herbert Schultze, was given leave to be with his wife, who was poorly after giving birth to twins; the boat then temporarily acquired other Kommandants.

Soon war broke out, and the practice patrols in the Atlantic became deadly serious. In the words of the song on everyone's lips at the time '. . . for we sail against England'. All boats now carried two watch-officers. Because there was a shortage of suitable personnel, they fell back on officers from the Crews from '34 back to '32, who were still in some respects novices. Nevertheless, being senior in length of service they were put in positions of 1WO over the heads of the others. However, it was decided that I shouldn't take a downwards step again, so I stayed as 1WO. The chief of my flotilla insisted on this, since I had got on well under all the Kommandants attached to him. The war didn't start overnight. It was preceded by the Memel and Sudetenland crises. The conflict over Poland, too, hung in the air. Poland, freed in the First World War from Russian domination by means of German arms, had acquired access to the Baltic by decree of the Western powers. This was the 'Polish corridor', that separated the province of Eastern Prussia from the Reich. Moreover, Poland had become involved in a war against the USSR, and even during peacetime had annexed the Lithuanian capital of Wilna by means of a coup. Polish insurgents had penetrated Oberschliessen, but had been driven back, due to German intelligence. The history of the Weimar Republic, all too little heeded, shows the strained relationship between Germany and Poland. The territorial targets of Poland lay far to the west, and they had entertained thoughts of a pre-emptive strike against the small German force of 100,000. The only thing that stopped these thoughts being put into action was the fact that Germany had to make reparation payments to the Allies, and England in particular didn't want to get entangled in a war which might have hindered these payments. By the same token, because of the growing power of Germany, England and France were induced in 1938 to ally themselves with Poland, who felt worried about the superiority of Germany. In 1936, the year of the Berlin Olympics, Poland had revoked the corridor agreement, and broken off all territorial agreements with Germany regarding Eastern Prussia. After the Hitler–Stalin pact, everything that followed was only a matter of time.

For many the war with England came out of the blue, though Dönitz had always voiced the opinion, 'If it should come to war in the end, England will be in it and on the opposite side from us!' However, that was in direct contradiction to what Adolf Hitler was supposed to have stated firmly to Großadmiral Raeder, the head of the navy: 'There is no question of a war against England'. But if that was supposed to be what he seriously thought, it just shows badly he had mis-

Großadmiral Raeder, Commander-in-Chief of the German Navy.

U-48 at Kiel – February 1940 (l–r) Hartung (ship-builder), 2WO Ites, 1WO Suhren, Kommandant Schultze, LI Zurn.

judged the British. They declared war on Germany. In the Kriegsmarine they were mainly concerned with their large and impressive warships. The submarine service seems to have been ranked bottom of the list, and we went into the Second World War with little more than fifty boats. Of these, forty-six were ready for action; moreover fewer still, to be precise twenty-two, were fit for the Atlantic. The relevant 'Rule of a Third' applied to the situation (namely a third in dock, and a further third on their way out or back). This meant that we were left with the modest remaining third of at the most seven boats ready for the Front. In reality it wasn't even as many as that.

These few boats had to circle all the way round England in order to take up their action-stations at the western end of the Channel. One of them was ours: *U-48*. As has already been mentioned, the Kommandant was Herbert Schultze. His nickname – 'Vati', or 'Daddy' – says it all. These first patrols of ours

U-48 at sea – May 1940. (Seated from r) Kommandant Rösing, 1WO Suhren, (standing from r) 2WO Ites, LI Zurn.

were particularly interesting, because we proceeded on the basis that we were obliged to carry on a war at sea according to 'Prize Rules'. These Prize Rules had been set up jointly with England. The British Admiral Sir John Fisher had stated at the first Hague Convention (1899), with reference to the conduct of naval engagements: 'As a representative of His Britannic Majesty I will sign all the prohibitions that anyone wishes me to sign; but as First Sea Lord of the British Fleet, in the event of war I shall try to achieve victory by any means at my disposal.' And already in the First World War it had become clear that in the long run it was impossible to wage a submarine war according to the Prize Rules. Modern communications and means of defence being what they were, one could hardly surface and coolly check every ship over for prohibited cargo. Nevertheless we did our best. The first freighter that crossed our path was a Swede. We closed in on him on the surface, and hoisted on the periscope the signal 'Stop at once! Do not use

Suhren examining the papers of a Swedish neutral (aboard *U-564*).

your radio!' The Swede acted as though he hadn't noticed. To show him we meant business, we gave orders to man the 8.8cm gun on the foredeck, and approached him at half-speed. The boat rolled in a slight swell, sea-state 3. When I looked over the bridge to give orders to the gun-crew, I saw there was no-one on the gun. The movement of the boat had swept them away. Fortunately they were clipped on with safety-harnesses and now hung suspended on ropes over the saddle-tanks. The Kommandant reacted immediately and stopped the boat so that they could pull themselves back on board. Gradually the Swede realised what was going on, and hove to. 'Vati' Schultze let him go as a neutral. One thing however we learnt from this: namely, that in the Atlantic, travelling at any sort of speed, and maybe even head-on to a sea, the gun is useless. One could only just manage to stay on one's feet if the sea was completely calm.

At midday the following day (it was 5 September and I'd just sent the Obersteuermann off watch down from the bridge), mastheads appeared again. The outline of an impressive ship appeared above the horizon: the British freighter *Royal*

Sceptre, a 5,000-tonner. The Kommandant ordered 'Dive!' We made ourselves scarce so as to surface just ahead of the freighter. All went exactly as planned. Signal: 'Stop at once and show papers!' The Kommandant gave the crew ten minutes to get into the boats. We couldn't hang about for long in this area, which was fraught with danger, without getting ants in our pants. From 600m distance the torpedoes hit amidships, and when the ship tried to send radio messages we fired a few shells at her. That was the end. 'Pity about the nice ship, Herr Kaleu'. 'Vati' Schultze nodded; 'Well, this war was none of my choosing.' Events come in pairs. The waves had scarcely closed over the *Royal Sceptre*, and their boats were bobbing about near us, when the look-out again reported, 'Freighter sighted ahead!' We laid a course towards it, and as soon as we could make out its name (it was the English freighter *Browning*, a 5,000-tonner of the Lamport and Holt line, out of Liverpool) it immediately sent boats to meet us. We couldn't believe our eyes when we heard a great wailing borne across on the wind. In the first boat sat stout 'black mommas', who were reaching up their little babies to us and howling fit to break a heart of stone. The tears ran down their faces. It was a heart-rending scene, as they pleaded for their lives and for their children. We weren't prepared for all that. What did they take us for? 'Vati' Schultze, who had a particularly kind heart and was very likely thinking of his own twins, looked at me helplessly, despite his determination as Kommandant. 'Good God, what on earth do we do now?' In my usual impulsive way I blurted out, 'No way am I prepared to torpedo it!' Schultze replied immediately, 'No more am I'. But what now? After a short pause for thought he announced. 'The poor things are quite obviously caught up in the war against their will. We'll send them back to their ship. They can pick up the survivors from the *Royal Sceptre* and carry on with their voyage.' Either my English wasn't of the best, or they were in a state of shock. Thinking that their hour had come they didn't at first dare go back on board for fear that we'd blow them sky-high. In vain did we try to make ourselves understood; they didn't trust us. But the moment we slowly turned away and shouted to them 'Don't make use of your radio!' they hurried to make their way back again; and across the water drifted loud and clear their spiritual, 'Jesus come back to me'. It all went according to plan. They didn't radio, continued on their course, and made it into port three weeks later in South America with the survivors of the *Royal Sceptre*.

After the sinking of the British freighter *Winkleigh* on 8 September we received orders to return home. As well as the *Winkleigh* we had just disposed of the British freighter *Firby*, also a 5,000-tonner. The Captain had come on board and was close to tears. We were very moved, particularly when we discovered the cause of his distress. Against his wife's advice he had taken his son on the trip and was now desperate that our boat should do something to help him. 'Take him with you,' he pleaded. With the best will in the world that wasn't possible under the circumstances, but 'Vati' Schultze hit on a solution. We sent out a plain-text radio-signal: 'To Mr Churchill – We just sank the British steamer *Firby*. Please safe (*sic*!) the crew!'– and added our latitude and longitude. Naturally this compassionate message got noticed, and the crew of the *Firby*, together with the Captain's son, were soon rescued by the British.

So we certainly thought twice before doing away with people who had got caught up in the war. We found ourselves caught up in quite remarkable situations, and rendered assistance wherever it was possible. This was all the subject of debate among submarine staff at Headquarters later, but we couldn't keep it up indefinitely. We said to ourselves, 'It's all very well, but it's not that easy. We have a war on our hands. The news must have got round by now. People will be keeping a sharp look-out – especially the enemy'. The enemy had indeed been warned to be on the look-out. The English Channel and other seaways were mined, a regular submarine patrol was set up, and the hunt was on for our few boats. And we too had to show that we took this seriously.

Our Kommandant, Kapitänleutnant Schultze, was a really kind-hearted man. On the way back on the occasion of our first assignment, we had a sick man on board. An engine mechanic was rolling about and groaning away in his bunk with stomach-ache. In response to questions he only whimpered. I couldn't make head nor tail of it. 'Vati' gave orders for one bunk in the officer's mess to be vacated; one of the WOs had to move out so that his bunk could become a make-shift sick-bay! 'Not me,' I explained with feeling – I couldn't stand this kind of playing for sympathy; there's no way I was prepared to make a sacrifice of that sort! So it was up to our Number 2, the noble Otto Ites. At first, it must be said, he protested feebly, 'But I need to get my beauty sleep too!' Then however he changed places. Every morning when I prodded the sick man a great wail arose – always the same! And 'Vati' Schultze sat there, beating up eggs in stout out of the kindness of his heart to make a special invalid's diet. What a nice man he was! Between the Orkneys and the Shetlands I had an idea. 'Otto', I said, ' As soon as the Obersteuermann goes on watch, we'll be alone in the mess. I'm going to start spinning a yarn about how dangerous it's getting. And we'll see how quickly our so-called invalid gives up your bunk.' And that was what happened. As Otto appeared in the mess, where the crewman was having a good sleep in the bunk, he noticed my worried expression. 'What's up, Teddy?' 'Otto', I muttered, with a sideways glance at the bunk, 'we're just entering the North Sea. There's trouble in store. Only 50m deep, and all mined. Just think of it; we've had a signal that Tommy has mined the whole North Sea. What if we cop it? I'm staying right here by the tower.' 'I'm coming right away too. I wouldn't fancy being left inside to drown if we hit a mine.' Pause. There were sounds of stirring in the bunk. Otto looked at me. 'You're right, Number 1', he answered anxiously. 'Where's my escape-gear? Best to put a lifejacket on too . . .' – and with that off we went. It wasn't long before we saw our invalid nimbly up and about, with lifejacket and escape-gear under his arm, standing in the control-room. He'd raised his eyes heavenwards to the main hatchways, obviously with an view to getting out! 'Look, Otto, now you can sleep in your own bunk again with a clear conscience'.

All the same, the journey back was not without its dangers. Headquarters had warned us of enemy submarines in the Kattegatt. The Kommandant therefore decided that the best way to go through the Kattegatt was in the dark and at full speed. Five of us were positioned on the bridge, the Old Man, both of us WOs, and the two senior hands. We even spotted the silhouette of an enemy boat, but before we could turn and try to ram her, she had vanished again. We reached Kiel unscathed. Iron Crosses all round.

On 1 October 1939 I became Oberleutnant zur See. The unrestricted submarine war had begun, and the blockade of England was intensified. In the same month other ships, both French and British, fell victim at sea to our torpedoes; they were picked off while in convoy by *U-48. Emile Miguet*, *Louisiane*, *Heronspool*, *Sneaton* and *Clan Chisholm*, altogether some 37,000 tons. *U-47*, under Kapitänleutnant Günther Prien, provided the sensation of the month. Engelbert Endrass was still 1WO on board. After meticulous planning by Dönitz himself the boat managed, on 13 October 1939, to break through into the British naval base of Scapa Flow in the Orkneys. As a result the battleship HMS *Royal Oak* was sunk, with a loss of life of 833 men and their Admiral. This undertaking, which was successful in the end despite a few set-backs, caused an enormous sensation and in one fell swoop brought home the importance of the submarine service. The whole crew of *U-47* were invited to Berlin, and the Kommandant, as senior officer on board, was decorated with the Knight's Cross. At the same time the FdU, Kapitän sur See Dönitz, was promoted to Admiral and 'Befehlshaber der U-boats' (BdU) (Commander of Submarines). It also served as good propaganda abroad, for the British casualties could not be hushed up: in the end the BBC broadcast the information worldwide.

Christmas was celebrated at sea, with a modest miniature tree in the forward torpedo room, on the so-called 'threshing-floor' – the false floor over the spare torpedoes. *U-48* was one of the Type VIIB boats. They weighed 760 tons, could cruise at 17 knots on the surface and had a considerable range. It made no difference that the boat was only 66.5m (218ft) long and 6m (20ft) broad overall; the crew of around fifty crawled around in the pressure-hull that was even shorter and narrower, and had the greatest difficulty in keeping out of each other's way. Eventually, though, we got used to the restricted space. From the bow-room for'ard to the diesel engines and the electric motor room aft which contained stern torpedo tube number 5, ran a direct narrow passageway. It was flanked by bunks, cables, valves and hand-wheels, tubes and instruments, radio apparatus and electric galley; it led past the WC and the spare WC and was divided by two bulkheads, with circular hatches in them that one had to stoop to clamber through. At the half-way point, hence right in the middle of the boat, was the control-room, with gyro-compass, the pits for the two periscopes (attack and air-search), the hand-operated valves for diving, horizontal and vertical hydroplanes and the other vital controls. Over the top was the bell-shaped tower, and the central hatch for getting out. Everything was crammed together in the smallest possible space, and was lit by electric lights, which reflected off the blue and oily steel. The tiny 'Captain's Cabin' was the only corner whose entrance was screened off by a simple curtain.

At the beginning of the patrol we were even more pushed for space. Bread was suspended in hammocks, long-life würsts hung down from the deckheads. In the toilets were stacked cans of preserves. Anyway – Guten Appetit! Although the crew quarters in the bow were the largest single area, that had to serve at the same time as torpedo storage space. In the bow itself were four torpedo tubes, for replacement torpedoes had to be carried. And because the boat took with it fourteen 'eels' on patrol, in the early days of a patrol it was absolutely crammed full. Some of the eels were stored under the floorboards, and torpedoes 11 and 12 above, on top of a wooden 'false floor,' the 'threshing-floor'

The limited crew-space aboard a U-boat (*U-564*).

already mentioned. This is where Christmas was celebrated, or perhaps one should say, imagined, in a crouching position. It was quite impossible during the day to lead any sort of a normal life in the forward torpedo room. Until at least one or two torpedoes had been fired, thereby making some room, the occupants couldn't even stand upright to change their clothes. And when we got ourselves into a tight spot which involved a lot of

Torpedoes were in constant need of adjustment when at sea.

twisting and turning, the boat pitched and tossed in the Atlantic and hurled us from one corner to another. Moreover, the steel 'eels' were complicated instruments, which had the special characteristic of needing to be pulled out of their tubes every few days – even those kept in reserve – to be checked by the torpedo men. If the one lying on the left underneath needed to be worked on, the next had to be moved out of the way up to the right, over the top, with a sort of chain-and-block arrangement. In any sort of sea, in the restricted space, it was a hard nut to crack, and got everyone into a sweat.

The sea is a vast area, and what they taught us in tactics still holds good: 'Vanish in the expanse of the Atlantic.' Our operational areas, though, lay next to each other, which was how it came to pass that on a grey overcast day towards the year's end we met up with *U-37*, a submarine from another flotilla under the command of Werner Hartmann. Two whales, bobbing about in the sea so that the water ran foaming from their flanks. On the bridge muffled figures, just silhouettes. I knew that my brother Gerd Suhren was on board – we were all aware of it. So it wasn't long before I spotted him on the bridge. We called inaudibly to each other. The wind tore the words from our lips, and all we had left were our wild gestures. Then we each went our separate ways, and lost sight of each other. Fate decreed that at that time we were the only boats stationed at the Front. All the others were on their way out or back, or in dry-dock. And it was a strange coincidence that my brother was serving in one boat as LI, and I was 1WO in the other. Then New Year arrived, and New Year was the time when the commanders of the various sections of the armed forces cooked up silly little messages to pass round the men under their command. Some joker on the staff of the BdU concocted an appropriate verse for the situation, though officially he was supposed to be sending out a message about something entirely different. It went out round everyone in the submarine service:

> *'Nur Mut, nur Mut –,*
> *Familie Suhren ist auf der Hut*
> *Und kämpft gegen England'*
> ('Take heart, take heart:
> The Suhren family is on the war-path,
> And fighting against England.')

That is how small our submarine service was.

5

Pinned down on the seabed – A Supershot – My 200,000 tons and the Knight's Cross

WE HAD OF COURSE LOSSES to lament as well. In the first half year a good dozen of our boats went missing. With them comrades were lost; among them was my old friend Jürgen, 1WO on *U-41*. On a blue-grey winter's day our boats had laid alongside one another in the harbour at Heligoland. We were on our way back from patrol, and they were wanting to get out there. Jürgen wore an unusually serious, even dejected expression. Shortly before, he had received the news that his elder brother, member of an aircrew, had been lost. In the course of our conversation he suddenly said without warning, 'Teddy, I have a feeling that I shan't be coming back either.' All attempts to reassure him were useless. Next morning he left on patrol. I never saw Jürgen again. *U-41* was sunk by escorts on 5 February 1940 after twice attacking a convoy bound for North America. He was absolutely right. There were no survivors . . .

For the submarines the war became harder. The Allies had armed their merchant ships, as in the First World War, and shot at anything which looked like a submarine. More importantly however they stuck them together in convoys, and gave them escort ships (destroyers, corvettes or armed fishing boats) to accompany them far out into the Atlantic, and others to take them over again at the opposite end. And though initially they were short of escorts, they still had more of them than we had submarines – and we couldn't make an omelette without breaking eggs.

Suhren at the main periscope of *U-564*.

The bad weather was a factor too. It seems sometimes as though years of war and catastrophe can actually influence the weather, and give everyone even more to worry about. The first winter of the war, 1939–40, was exceptionally hard. The Kiel Canal was frozen over, and we could only get through the Northern Baltic canal with the help of an icebreaker. On both sides of the channel lay ice floes piled yards high on top of each other, and we wore a 'bow-cap' so as not to dent our nose. The North Sea was in the grip of devilish cold weather. The oilskins of the bridge-watch iced over with the spray. The drops of water remained hanging in eyebrows and beards, and turned to ice immediately. Binoculars held in a gloved fist misted over when you held them in front of the eyes. Nevertheless we had to be on the alert so as not to be taken unawares by enemy planes. Inside the boat everything was damp. The electric heaters were no use against the cold. Condensation glistened on the bulkheads, and one's breath hung in the air like a fog. It was a losing battle trying to dry our wet clothes; we even tried hanging up our underpants in the fug of the engine-room. Our leather outer clothes absolutely refused to dry. In order to build up a bit of warmth in my bunk at least, I put on two complete sets of underclothes. It didn't help much, and we dozed rather than slept properly.

During these months *U-48* sank sixteen ships totalling over 100,000 tons. In the course of it we also mined Portland Harbour on the other side of the Channel. We approached it through thick fog from the west, that is, from the opposite end. We were flying completely blind; we could hardly see our hands in front of our faces. It got even worse when out of the blue the high silhouette of an aircraft-carrier dashed past us and suddenly vanished again. Just when we were thinking about postponing the mission, suddenly the fog lifted and the Portland light came into view, so we could take a bearing and get our mines away. As far as I know, two freighters fell victim to them later.

All our assignments went off better than expected, until one time when we crossed, south of Ireland, over to the St George's and Bristol Channels, and got quite a shock; we were just about literally knocked for six . . . Out of the morning mist loomed the outlines of ships. A large convoy was coming straight for us. 'Kapitän, on the bridge! Alarm! Crew to action stations' The boat dives with a roar and sinks to periscope-depth. The keel is now 14m under the surface. Zürn, the LI, trims the boat. Everything hangs in the balance; from this moment on, success and even the fate of the boat depend on the Kommandant. 'Vati' Schultze takes a look round, then lowers the periscope, lifts it up again, puts the right pedal down and swings automatically through 360 degrees. He's up in the conning-tower, I'm underneath him in the control-room, and make sure that his orders are properly carried out. The front caps of the torpedo tubes are opened. Without raising his voice, the Kommandant speaks with his No 1 who is on the TDC, the torpedo-attack computer. This apparatus transfers the course-angle down through the tubes to the adjustors on the torpedoes; these are air-driven gyros which start up as the torpedo is fired and steer the torpedo in the right direction. In the boat everyone is as quiet as a mouse. Only the electric motors which drive the boat underwater, are humming quietly. We are travelling slow-ahead. The air is full of tension. Engine and rudder orders come more frequently. I stick my head up through the hatch. 'OK, chief?' 'Vati' nods; 'We're standing well off to port; in five minutes I'll be ready to shoot.' Question; 'Much in the way of escorts?' 'Vati' nods; 'Enough!' The Kommandant puts up the periscope again and takes a look round. 'Tubes one to four, stand by! Tube one – fire! Tube two – fire! Three – fire! Four – fire!'

The LI is having difficulty keeping the boat at periscope-depth now, and requests more speed. The distance to the enemy target is about 1,800m, the torpedoes do 30 knots. The stopwatch ticks away. In 120 seconds we should hear a bang. '80 seconds up', reports the Obersteuermann. 80 – 100 – 110! The Kommandant gives orders to turn to starboard. Then – a dull thud. Bull's-eye! 'Quick, go deep!' 'Why, what's up?' 'An escort's spotted us; she's coming straight at us!' Things happen fast. Two further explosions indicate further hits. *U-48* dives flat out. At 120m, eight depth-charges shake us, one after the other. They are pretty accurate. We lurch this way and that, and move at a crawl. Then we can clearly hear the enemy asdic; ping, ping, ping! He's pinned us down good and proper. From

The electric motors were mainly used for travelling when submerged.

the engine-room comes a report: 'Exhaust valves making water!' The Kommandant orders, 'Zürn, see to it that the valves are closed down as far as they'll go.' Zürn reports back that despite all their continuing efforts we're still shipping a small amount of water. Now the ear has to take over from the eye. In our hydrophones the rumble of the departing convoy decreases. The propeller noise of the destroyers drowns it out. It is just 07.00. The propeller noises move past over us and sound like a long fingernail scraping on a dinner-plate. Right away I pick up the faint bubbling sound of falling depth-charges; then I give the radio-operator the headphones back. The charges are about to go off. An explosion, hard as steel, above us, and then five more in succession. Peng-wamm! The Kommandant changes course to the west.

07.30. The next attack. The boat drops to 120m. At 08.00 the next attack, each time five charges. The explosions are getting closer. At 135m there is a bump. The Kommandant stops engines. The boat has landed on the seabed. The charts put us on the Cockburn Bank. A destroyer is still creeping around up above us, looking for us. Ping, ping, ping! Propeller noises nearby, and the gentle bubbling of depth-charges. Peng-wamm, peng-wamm, peng-wamm! The bombs go off amidships, over our heads, and make the boat shake like a steel feather. Bow and stern jerk about, and the 800-ton boat is tossed metres up in the water and bounces back down again onto the seabed. Twice, three times. It shakes every joint in the boat. We can scarcely stay on our feet; we look for a handhold and hang on wherever we can.

Inside it's deathly quiet now. The slightest sound – a tiny bit of metal falling on the deckplates – scares the wits out of us. The man responsible gets an angry stare from everyone. You can read the build-up of tension in the faces of the crew. They all hang on tight. There have already been eleven attacks with five charges each. It's coming up to midday, but no-one is bothered about lunch. One wonders what might be passing through the minds of the crew. The Obersteuermann is married, with two children. He must find it hard. I mutter to him, 'Depth-charges sink at 4m per second; perhaps the listening-room can pick up the smack as they're thrown overboard, then we can use the stop-watch to time how long they take to explode and work out the depth-setting they're using.' The listening-room thinks it should be able to pick up the splash. As the destroyer runs in again, and we are about to be subjected to the next hail of depth-charges, they are on the alert and give the start-time to the Obersteuermann. He clicks on the stop-watch – 'How long?' '28 seconds to detonation!' It's repeated five times. So – 110–120 metres. However, that's the deepest that English depth-charges can be set to explode, and should be our salvation. Small comfort – after all, we're worryingly close to this limit. But I'm relieved for the moment. The Kommandant asks me, 'What do you think? Should we leak out a bit of oil? Then they'd be sure to think they'd hit us.'

But I shake my head. 'No, no movement at all; just play dead. Once it gets dark, they'll knock it off.' It's at least six hours till then. We must get some sleep, like Otto Ites. The 2WO is lying in his bunk with his face to the wall, and seems not to have a care in the world. What nerves the man has!

Gently I feel my way to the forward torpedo room, where the crew sprawl open-eyed, or squat on the floor with their bowed heads supported in both hands. The torpedo-mate has wedged himself in between the tubes, as if to protect himself against further shocks. I had hoped to lift a heavy weight from the hearts of the crew with the news about the English depth-charges exploding too far above us, and thought that they would be able to comfort themselves with this thought until darkness fell; but I see that I'm sorely mistaken. Here and there is an incredible twisted smile. The 'sealords', normally so alert, are staring ahead and waiting for the end. I am optimistic myself though, even if they do carry on firing at us. And Otto Ites sticks just his head out of his bunk: 'How much more of Churchill's little bag of tricks are they proposing to throw at us?' But it's more of a statement than a question. The LI can't leave the control-room, and so he asks me to have a word with the men in the engine-room to cheer them up by telling them the fairy-tale (as he puts it) of the depth-charges which can only detonate up to a depth of 120m. He can't imagine it himself. Only 'Vati' Schultze is a picture of calm – and that's ultimately what decides the state of the crew, and prevents them from cracking up.

All are resting, even the escorts. That's the most useful thing one can do. No unnecessary movement, no rapid breathing; we must conserve air. The ventilator is running and pumps out oxygen-enriched air into all the compartments while at the same time sucking out the stale air through the CO_2 filter. Its hissing grates on all our nerves, but that can't be avoided. And the Englishman doesn't give up the attack. He is persistent, and he knows what he's doing. Every half-hour he passes over us and depth-charges us; the noise is terrific. We wonder whether we would have had so much patience, or whether we'd already have reported 'enemy destroyed'. Gradually my doubts return. How long can an execution take?

A U-boat undergoes a depth-charge attack.

The hours pass painfully slowly. It must have got dark long ago on the surface. The hands of the clock indicate 22.00. And again – propeller noises over our head. This time eight depth-charges go off. What does this different number mean? Is it a farewell gesture? Have they finally shot their bolt? 'Listening-room, what can you hear?' 'Herr Oberleutnant, I can hear the two destroyers getting further away!' I report to the Kommandant that according to their bearing they seem to be headed off in the direction of the Bristol Channel. 'Suhren, I'll sit it out for another half-hour. If nothing further happens, then I'll give orders to start the pumps'. 'Chief, wouldn't it be better to blow tanks and get back on the surface again?' 'No, Suhren, we've got water in the boat weighing us down. We've got to get rid of it first; then it'll go up more easily.'

The half-hour is up. It's still quiet, nothing stirs above us. After a little while the Kommandant gives orders to start the pumps. The pumps have a hard job against the pressure of 13.5 atmospheres outside; their high-pitched humming threatens to drive me round the bend. And so another three-quarters of an hour passes. If the enemy picks up a whisper of it, we'll be in deep trouble all over again. Slowly, slowly, the boat loses weight, and gradually it lifts, barely struggling off the seabed. We rise.

The pumps are knocked off and at 100m the Kommandant goes slow ahead with the electric motors. 'Suhren, as soon as we break surface, we'll nip up onto the bridge. I'll take the starboard side. You follow on immediately behind and take a look to port.' 'Jawohl, Chief.' The tower breaks surface, the hatch flies open. It makes the eardrums ache with the equalising of pressure – and all of a sudden we're out in the open air. Bright lights flicker to starboard and to port. We are encircled by about twenty fishing boats which are lying at anchor. Behind us on the Cockburn Bank two buoys with lights mark our supposed resting place. But nothing is stirring. The night is still. With the boat half-submerged and only the conning-tower above water, we use a touch of the e-motors to steer for the largest gap between the shadows. Soon we leave them behind us; we are free. Another 1,000m, then the sound of the diesels starting up; we make a quick getaway. Thank God we're still alive! The bridge watch is set up, and one of them is Otto Ites. He clasps my hand impulsively. 'That didn't half have me worried there, No 1'. Taken aback, I reply, 'What, Otto? You too? And there was I thinking you were peacefully asleep!' 'No, no; it just looked like that.' Well, no-one is fearless; even the strongest can fall flat on their backsides sometimes.

Scarcely had we sorted ourselves out again when new shadows loomed up astern and quickly get closer. We report to the Kommandant, 'Torpedoes ready!' 'Vati' Schultze goes in to attack the middle freighter. Target-computer running; torpedo away. An explosion after 1,200m. And with this bulls-eye the tension that has built up vanishes and bursts like a soap-bubble. 'There you are, Suhren; attacking again and getting a hit are the best medicine. And now, let's see about getting the others lined up – and step on the gas. Come on, up and at 'em!' Sadly, I miss – one shouldn't tempt Providence too far!

During the dropping of the depth-charges, which went off over our heads while we had to sit there patiently and helplessly, I found myself thinking back to Germania-Werft in Kiel, and to the workmen who had built our boat. At the core of it was the pressure hull, which contained all the elements essential for operating: in short, it was the world within which we survived underwater. It consisted of steel a good 20mm thick, that could withstand water-pressure up to 250m deep. Because of the intense water-pressure it was not riveted but welded; and if the welding had given way and split only in a single place, the water would have shot in with unimaginable power; the smallest leak would have been impossible to stop. We would have had to surface. Under normal circumstances the pressure hull would have been able to withstand diving to 250m, and even a bit more than that; after that, however, as the water pressure increased further, it would have been crushed like an eggshell.

All's well that ends well. We made five patrols with 'Vati' Schultze and sank 100,000 tons. On 2 March 1940 he became

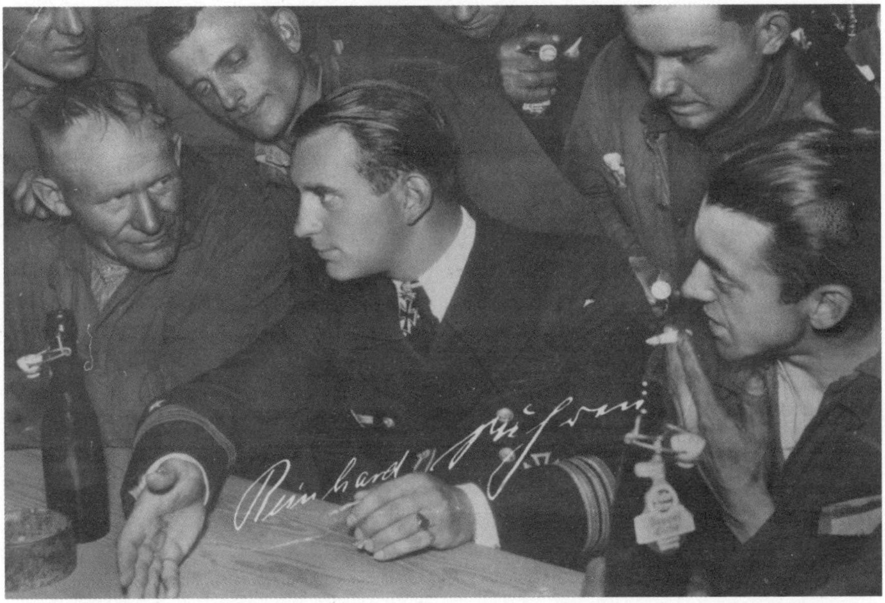

Germania-Werft was the shipyard responsible for building most of the U-boats. Suhren is shown here with some of the workers.

the first Submarine Kommandant after Prien to get the Knight's Cross to the Iron Cross. I was awarded the Iron Cross 1st Class. Our last patrol was connected with the invasion of Norway. We first stood off the Shetland Isles and then were directed to Narvik to support our land-offensive. The main German operational force consisted of ten destroyers, a full third of our total, who had dropped off the Gebirgsjäger, the special mountain troops, at Narvik under General Dietl after a stormy crossing. While running into a fjord we encountered a destroyer. At this point there was a difference of opinion between Schultze and myself. 'Vati' took the warship for a German destroyer; I was doubtful about it, had another look, and then strongly disagreed with him; 'As a Fähnrich I served on a destroyer, and I know what German ones look like. This is a true-blue Englander!' The Kommandant said, 'Well, give him the recognition signal.' I disagreed; 'What for? We need to dive, the quicker the better!' Since I was still adamant,

Schultze reluctantly gave way, for the destroyer had already got pretty close; it lay diagonally across from us, and had pointed all its guns at us. We dived just as the depth-charges fell around us! Schultze was furious: 'And you're to blame for us getting all those German depth-charges on our heads.' I retorted, 'Those aren't German depth-charges, they're English; they sound so loud because we're lying here in the narrow fjord and the sound echoes off the steep sides.'

After the eighth charge, I said casually, on a hunch, 'If he's English, he'll chuck another five at us. Today is Friday April 13, and Tommy will throw thirteen depth-charges; just you see, Chief!' 'Vati' Schultze looked at me as though I was pulling his leg and it was all rubbish. But as it happened the destroyer dropped another five and moved on. Further up the fjord, just about in sight of the town, we met up with another German submarine – *U-46* (Herbert Sohler). We cruised on the surface, and he called across to us, 'Boys, just watch out. In Narvik there isn't a single German destroyer left; all ten have been sunk by the English. It's swarming with English destroyers,

Salvaging stores from a destroyer sunk at Narvik.

and what's more, the battleship *Warspite* is there with them!' 'Vati' Schultze didn't say another word.

The invasion of Norway had been a disaster from the navy's point of view; but we too suffered a different and inexplicable set-back. All the submarines stationed there made a number of attacks against the English navy; but they were completely unsuccessful. Whether the target was a cruiser, a battleship or a destroyer, we seemed not to be able to hit anything, but shot straight past them. The problem lay not in the shooting, but something much more serious. The torpedoes were misfiring. The e-torpedo G7e carried a remote trigger that was supposed to be set off by the magnetic field of the target, but it didn't work properly. So there was a concrete reason for our lack of success. We were to discover that later, but at the time we were faced with a puzzle that caused a lot of disquiet among submarine personnel.

We were worried one day by a dreadful and inexplicable noise that we picked up underwater in the fjord. Though we knew that the banks of the comparatively small fjord reflected every sound underwater and magnified it, this booming and whistling, which got steadily louder, was something we'd never heard before; an unknown hazard! Automatically we went down deep, held our breath, and felt something inexorably approaching. The noise got louder and louder and ever more threatening, and turned eventually into a racket that drowned out everything in the boat. 'This is the end', we thought, 'they've got us now.' The LI ran up to me and opened his mouth, but I couldn't understand a word, and in desperation could only swear back at him. I was beyond caring. Then when all seemed to be lost, the deafening racket started to decrease, got quieter and quieter and faded into the distance. Incredulously we looked at each other. What on earth had been going on? Much later I got to the bottom of it. By then I was Kommandant of *U-564*, and was making a dummy attack for practice on our own battleship the *Bismarck*. I was 30m down; and there it was again, that droning noise that, I have to admit, had put the fear of God into us in Norway. It was the propeller-noise of the gigantic battleship, its three propellers grinding through the water like three huge egg-whisks. That time in the fjord it had been the old English battleship the *Warspite*, that had gone past over our heads. Anyway, it was soon over and done, just a passing incident.

After Narvik, Kapitänleutnant Schultze was taken ill, and was relieved by Hans-Rudolf Rösing. Rösing belonged to the Crew of '24, and had seen the establishment of the submarine service from its beginnings. He was over thirty-five years old. His father had formerly been a naval officer, and his father-in-law was Konteradmiral Looff, the one whose cruiser *Königsberg* was shot to pieces off German East Africa in the First World War. His brother-in-law likewise served in the submarine service. It was with Rösing that Otto Ites and I did the seventh and eighth patrols of *U-48*. Rösing was a reflective fellow, very sensitive, and during underwater attacks, when the greatest concentration was required from the Kommandant, the sweat used to run in rivers down his face. But he stuck to his guns. Coming as he did from a line of naval officers, he had highly-developed ideals of courage and heroism which over-rode everything else. I developed the greatest respect for this man; for he needed greater self-control than someone with a naturally thicker skin. Needless to say he made a very pleasant and courteous Kommandant. With him we sank fourteen ships, around 80,000 tons.

Under Rösing the episode of the 'Supershot' occurred. Before we get to it, I ought to say some more about shooting, and in particular about setting up an attack. Principally we attacked by night and on the surface, since a boat on the surface could cruise at a maximum of 17 knots on diesels. Once below the surface, it could only creep around at about 7 knots with the help of the motors, so was less manoeuvrable and easier to catch up with. While the silhouettes of high-sided freighters just about towered to the sky when we looked at them from below, it was surprising how we could quite easily look down on smaller boats. At night the dark boat blended in with the dark of the sea. Just occasionally we would leave a phosphorescent wake behind us, but that didn't happen as often as all that; so by the time the enemy realised what was going on below them, the fat was usually already in the fire. The older and more experienced kommandants would close in to more or less a stone's-throw away from their target so that there was a better chance of hitting it. Underwater attacks are carried out single-handed by the Kommandant, and he does the shooting himself. In the case of surface-attacks the shooting is left to the torpedo officer, mostly to the 1WO. He takes a bearing through the range-finder on the bridge, a high-powered pair of binoculars with a graduated scale attached. In order to hit the target, he estimates the distance, course and speed of the enemy, combines these with the bearing and works out from the target 'triangle' the angle at which the torpedo must run, either diagonally to meet the ship or from astern so as to catch up with it. It is vital to keep the boat absolutely still at the moment of making observations; it mustn't move at all, otherwise the angle will vary. It's a bit like the old still-photographers of our grandfather's day; on the command 'Smile, please!', one had to stand completely motionless, or the picture would blur. I always used to request the Kommandant just before firing, 'Rudder amidships, please!'

Success depended on precise computations. Of course the Kommandant put in his penny-worth, for in principle shooting is a joint operation. He might say. 'The course should be different,' or, 'It's cruising a bit faster', or even 'You haven't a clue . . .!' But when it's a matter of dealing with an experienced torpedo officer, everyone shuts up and lets him get on with it without interruption – even the Kommandant! The torpedo officer snatches a last glance through the sights at the target, then comes the order, 'Stand by – torpedo – fire!'

If it's a hit, everyone's happy – it's a lovely day! If it misses, then all those who had previously kept their mouths shut descend on him: 'We thought as much, but of course we didn't want to say anything . . .' But by dint of the fact that the firing of the torpedoes is the single most important operation on board, one is better off leaving it to an expert. Kommandants trusted me, and rarely interfered with what I was doing. On one occasion 'Vati' Schultze shouted incredulously, 'My God, you haven't hit it!' I was absolutely amazed; 'I don't know what the problem is either'. Then he had a go at shooting, and couldn't hit the target either. That was the first occasion that we had doubts about the reliability of the torpedoes . . .

Underwater the Kommandant had to do everything on his own – both control the boat and shoot. Instead of the open-air rangefinder, he used the attack periscope. He would go in, surface, take a look around, and do his sums; he couldn't hang about for long making up his mind. He had to rely largely on instinct and feeling. He had to concentrate on not being heard, always a difficult task for anyone. And if he overlooked a tiny detail, then we could end up getting rammed by the enemy. We never attacked underwater by night; the attack periscope simply didn't gather enough light. But by day it really wasn't easy to keep an eye on everything. I remember once when we were taken by surprise off Narvik by a destroyer coming from zero degrees – dead ahead. The Kommandant hadn't seen it. I tapped the LI on the shoulder and put my thumb down – that meant, 'Dive!' He lost no time in going down deep, and before the Kommandant knew what was going on, we were already at 50m. Not a second too soon; the depth-charges went off, fast and furious.

Then the 'Supershot' episode occurred. We got a big tanker lined up; it was in the distance and travelling fast. It would have been impossible to try to intercept it or catch it up, so – 'Eels at the ready!' The Kommandant had reservations. 'Suhren, are you serious about shooting? It's much too far away. Don't be a fool!' I replied, 'Herr Kaleu, don't let's waste time talking about it; if we don't get the torpedo off soon, the opportunity will slip through our fingers'. He retorted, 'At that distance you've no chance of hitting it!' I answered, 'Well, that's your opinion. I estimate distance at 5,000m, which the torpedo will cope with nicely'. I passed down the figures I worked out. Just before firing, at the very last moment, I increased the angle by 0.6 degrees. Yes – by 0.6! Then, 'Fire!' – and we sent off our little parcel at 30 knots. And no-one believed we would hit it. The tension grew. The seconds ticked away – one minute – two minutes – three minutes – four minutes: and that is an interminable length of time when you've taken a bit of a chance and are poised on tenterhooks! The rest of the crew cleared their throats, grinned furtively and turned away. Rösing shrugged his shoulders in a resigned sort of way, as if to say, 'What did I say? A waste of time.' Then after 5 minutes, and 4,900m, suddenly in the distance we saw an enormous fireball, and following it heard the sound of the explosion – a hit! The look-outs were dumbstruck, the 2WO looked up at me from below, flabbergasted. Rösing shook his head, gave me a quizzical sideways look, and silently left the bridge whilst the ship burnt like a torch in the distance. It was like something from *Der Freischütz.* They all had to eat their words. The 2WO said to the LI, 'I bet he couldn't do that again; it was a fluke'. 'Either it was a fluke, or he knows more about shooting than we do.' Later in the officers' wardroom (that's only a way of referring to it; it was just an area by the main passageway), he asked me frankly: 'Tell me, No 1, why did you increase the angle by 0.6 degrees at the last moment? That's the only reason we managed to hit it!' I replied, deadpan, 'The enemy had increased speed.' Otto said doubtfully, 'And could you actually tell that from here?' 'Dear Otto, don't be silly; just listen to me. At the last moment I noticed that the angle of 20.4 degrees wasn't divisible by 7. And because I've found that we've only scored hits when we've used numbers divisible by 7, I rounded it up, which brought it up to 21 degrees. And that just worked out right at that distance – believe it or not!' Otto said, 'You're barmy!' I retorted, 'It's not for a 2WO to tell a 1WO that he's barmy. Did I or didn't I hit it?' 'Yes, you did indeed – and that's all one can say!' Yes, that was all one could say. But the Kommandant never queried my judgement again.

Rösing tended to be a very persistent man, and was always reluctant to give up. I remember one occasion when we had shot everything except the torpedo in the stern tube. Meanwhile we were standing just off the English coast, and Otto and I were none too happy about the situation. By this time Otto and I didn't need to say much to each other. A gentle nudge on this occasion was enough – which meant, 'Otto, let's be off – fast!' Otto started to shout 'Destroyer, destroyer, dead ahead – we must move!' And off we went, with the last torpedo still in the tube.

Otto and I made two patrols with KK Rösing, in the course of which we sank fourteen ships. After Rösing, Heinrich Bleichrodt took over command of the boat. By now it was September 1940; the invasion of France was over, and we were now provided with submarine bases actually on the Atlantic coast. This was very useful, since it spared us the long preliminary approach round the British Isles. Our operational area was directly in front of us. *U-48* was transferred to Brest, with the 1st Flotilla. Bleichrodt was no natural submariner. He was one of the Crew of '31, and had done training trips under another Kommandant. These 'trainee-Kommandants' were popularly known as 'Confirmands'; the long and the short of it was that they were lacking in experience. So it was with Bleichrodt. There was no doubt that he had his weak spots as well as moments when he was not in control of events. That was to be expected. But Otto Ites was now travelling with us permanently – that is, for seven long patrols – and he was an old hand at the job. We two understood each other like brothers, and this needs to be borne in mind to understand what follows. Otto Ites liked best to travel through the middle of a group of ships, close enough to touch them with his hand. For reasons of tactics I wasn't so keen on this. Hence what happened: it was a pitch-black night, and when the watches changed, Otto relieved me. However, instead of keeping a proper look-out we started chatting, and before we realised what was happening we suddenly found ourselves in front of the middle column of a convoy. Only by putting the rudder hard across and revving the engines hard did we manage to avoid hitting them. As usual came the cry, 'Kommandant to the bridge!' In front of us a gap had opened up, through which we could have got out; we would then have been able to shoot accurately at the convoy from outside it. But Bleichrodt who had just been woken up could only see the side of a ship, tall as a house, and near enough to touch. He misjudged the situation and shouted, in a moment of panic, 'Alarm! Dive!' And with that, any chance we had of attacking went out of the window; it was too late. Otto just about fell into the control room in his haste to get below, and started to complain bitterly to the Kommandant, who was pulling the hatch to behind us. I was just ahead of the Kommandant and below him; I grabbed Otto by the collar and whispered, 'Shut up! Have you taken leave of your senses? Do you want to wreck the boat?' For if the crew's trust in the Kommandant is shaken, there's no telling what might happen. Otto shut up, his outburst of temper over. But the crew had picked up everything, and when we went ashore there were mutterings – 'Well, now then, . . .' This was the last thing I wanted, because I was going to have to face a de-brief from the Flotilla Chief. But I couldn't land my commanding officer in it, so to speak, and I played the whole thing down. Which was quite right and proper – after all, he'd always been very decent to us. We soon just about managed to compensate for his lack of experience, which was hardly his fault.

Well, even Bleichrodt got the hang of it in due course, and sank seventeen ships in the eighth and ninth patrols, ships on whose cargo Great Britain was dependent if she was not to starve or bleed to death. Altogether the boat was credited with forty-seven hits. Among them were modern freighters, tubs that were scarcely worth insuring, ships carrying mineral ore, colliers, fast ships and old globe-trotters, shabby tramps and gleaming liners. Few were alone; most were shot while in convoy. Whether armed, or unarmed neutrals, they had risked danger and perished because of it; they were all just ships, whose wakes stretched from one horizon to another. We could look them up with their dates and features in Naval Handbook No. 123, 'Merchant Fleets of the World'. It also contained their silhouettes, so that we could identify them if their radio messages gave nothing away and we couldn't read their names either. No matter whether they were called *Sultan Star*, or *Violande N Goulandris*, *Athelcrest* or *Port Gisborne*. Names were completely irrelevant; it was their tonnage that mattered. We did our best to shoot at everything we came across; indeed on our eighth and ninth patrols that was as many as four in a day. Reckoned altogether, within thirteen months that came to 300,000 tons of enemy shipping. That meant that we were talking about an average size of about 6,000 tons, corresponding to the normal-sized ship of the times; so this required countless approaches. When one considers that the supertankers and bulk goods carriers of today weigh as much as 200,000 to 300,000 tons, our end results don't seem that impressive in view of all the effort that went into it. In those days if one achieved 40,000 tons one earned a mention in despatches. And all Kommandants were keen to be mentioned in despatches.

A Knight's Cross was awarded to Kommandants who had sunk approximately 100,000 tons. Rösing got it, and Bleichrodt got his too. When the award of the Knight's Cross had been announced over the boat's radio, he telegraphed back – 'For who?' At the end of the patrol he stood there facing the BdU, to receive the decoration from Dönitz in person. (That was in Kerneval, at Lorient where the BdU had stationed his staff in order to be on the Atlantic coast near the boats.) Bleichrodt, who was quite a character, said to Dönitz, 'I can only accept this on one condition, Herr Admiral'. Dönitz was taken aback. 'What is that?' Bleichrodt explained. ' I'll accept mine provided that my 1WO, Suhren, gets his KC as torpedo

Gerd (L) and Teddy Suhren, both Knight's Cross winners.

officer; otherwise, no.' Admiral Dönitz in reply turned to Engelbert Endrass, who by then was a Kommandant, and said 'Well, Bertel, what do you say to that?' And Endrass replied, with his broad accent, 'Only one thing to do, Herr Admiral. Why shouldn't Suhren have the Knight's Cross too? I reckon he deserves it.' 'But he's still only a torpedo officer, and by rights should only get it after his first patrol as Kommandant'. 'Yes, but suppose he cops it before then, then that's it for his KC; he's got nowt to show for it.' And because Endrass was on good terms with Dönitz, and Dönitz took notice of what he said, he happily agreed. 'OK then, let him have it.'

But first I had to specify exactly how many freighters I had sunk as torpedo officer, and as a result of this the majority of *U-48*'s 300,000 tons of shipping were credited to me – in fact, 200,000 tons. So, on 4 November 1940 the KC was awarded to me, with the citation – '. . . because he played a decisive role in the sinking of 200,000 tons of enemy shipping' – which was something I could be very proud of; for I was the only submarine officer ever to be so decorated while still a WO. And the 200,000 tons continued to be credited to me later. Funny how things even out; just before that my brother Gerd Suhren, LI on *U-37*, had been the first engineer officer to be awarded the KC! It did indeed run in the family. But being realistic about it, the awards didn't just fall into our laps. We had to work for them, and to do a lot of shooting. Still, many hands make light work, and since the beginning of the war a large number of our boats had been continuously in action.

Even at that time, however, I was dogged by my past, and held back by an incident which was pretty typical; and its sequel spoke volumes. We young officers were all in our early twenties, and looked death in the eye every day at sea; and we weren't always on our best behaviour in port. Shortly before the Norwegian campaign – it was winter, and very cold – I had got into a bit of a argument, to put it mildly, at Holst's Hotel in the Schloßgarten at Kiel. The porter refused to let me into a room in which some of my mates were having dinner. One of them had managed to track down something to eat, and I wanted to join them. Now Kiel, unlike Wilhelmshaven, is no Navy town. They were always quite happy to take our money, but sailors were always 'coolies' as far as the townspeople were concerned – which was where the title of Theodor Pluvier's novel *The Kaiser's Coolies* came from. Things hadn't changed much in our time. For no obvious reason except pure cussedness the porter wouldn't let me join my mates, and was insolent with it. I said, 'Listen, I'll give you something to chew on in a minute . . .'. The man I'd been addressing rang the bell, and out came the hotelier, a well-known Kiel gastronome, bringing a side-kick with him, an equally well-known Kiel lawyer. And just at that moment my mates were coming down from upstairs and saw what was going on. Hein Uphoff whispered to me, 'Teddy, don't hit him, don't hit him!' The hotelier got all excited, and the lawyer shouted 'I'm going to ring my friend Admiral Carls!' They spoke together; then the lawyer surfaced again, and one of my mates drawled, 'What did your friend the Admiral say?' – and landed one on him which sent him flying into the cloakroom. And we were all in full uniform. Uphoff kept whispering to me, 'Stay out of it, Teddy, you're in enough trouble already . . .'.

Well, alas, things took their inevitable course. The lawyer drafted a statement about the whole incident. And correspondence about it shadowed me during all the months while I was off shooting torpedoes – it went from commanding officer to commanding officer, from Admiral to Admiral, with comments and official seals, until eventually it landed on the desk of the BdU. And the question was, what Dönitz would do now, and more importantly whether he would be able to get us off the hook. But the matter just about resolved itself of its own accord, in a tragic and macabre way. We were still at war, and among other things Dönitz could only answer, 'There is no longer any point in concerning yourself with submariners. Most of them are no longer with us . . .'.

6

No Kommandant under twenty-five – Happy Birthday, U-564 – The Abwehr is after me – Rum, and off to war

HANS-GEORG FRIEDEBURG WAS 2nd Admiral of Submarines as well as our personnel-officer. He had once been an officer in charge of cadets on a training-cruiser, and had belonged to the BI, for which I still harboured a deep resentment; nevertheless, we had built up a friendly relationship, and I never failed to report to him on board the *Erwin Wasser* in Kiel after I had returned from a patrol. He was in charge of all the postings, and it was as well to keep in his good books. Naturally he was aware of my reprehensible conduct, and contemplated me from under bushy eyebrows, part amused, part disapproving, but by and large benevolent.

The KC was hung round my neck by him personally, with many good wishes. I was to be transferred from *U-48*, but when I chose a suitable moment to ask about my next posting, and asked whether I could have my own boat, he brushed the request away in amazement. 'But my dear Suhren, what can you be thinking of? Your own boat? Do you know how many there are in the queue before you? Don't mention it again, and be off home. And besides, I won't have anyone as Kommandant under twenty-five years old.'

I was only twenty-four, and had to wait my turn in the queue, to my disappointment. Oh well, it obviously went by age rather than by experience. But I would have thought that after nine successful patrols as 1WO I could have done a better job than someone with less experience who was only being given a command because of his age.

Friedeburg again on the matter: 'The Lion (by which he meant Dönitz) has ordered that no-one under twenty-five can become a Kommandant.' Me: 'But in six months I'll be twenty-five; surely you could give me a boat now – why not?' 'No, that's not possible. I have my orders, and I cannot alter them.' 'So where am I supposed to go to carry on as a WO again?' Something in my voice must have got through to him. He shook his head. 'There's no point in discussing it. But I've got something even better for you. In Memel there is a torpedo course running, and we need an instructor there.' 'But that doesn't make sense', I countered, 'I'm only a WO so far, and I can't act as a teacher to Kommandants; they'd never take it from me.' Then Friedeburg grew fatherly: 'Listen to me, Suhren, they'll take it from you, believe me; they know who got a KC for his expert torpedo shooting. And after Memel, in six months time, we'll speak again.' He probably meant after I'd sobered up a bit; for naturally when one gets a decoration round one's neck a celebration is in order . . .

When I arrived at my new posting my boss, Kapitänleutnant Buchholz, welcomed me with open arms, and immediately said, 'Cheerio! I have orders to go to Berlin, so you take over here!' So quite unexpectedly I was not just a shooting-instructor, but in command as well. Not only did I introduce contemporaries of mine and members of older crews to shooting, but I even managed to help them become expert at it. We saw virtually nothing of Germany's easternmost sea-port and the surrounding countryside. The days were getting shorter. We sailed out in two little 250-ton submarines which were nicknamed 'canoes', and carried out practice attacks on the target ship, the Stettin passenger steamer *Nordland*. The torpedoes had practice warheads and passed under their targets; at the end of their run they were picked up by a 'catcher ship'. Top of the agenda came the difficult task of shooting by day underwater, which demanded the greatest concentration. The exercise required one to approach to a distance of between 600 and 800m without being seen. So as not to give away the position of the boat the periscope was only be raised above water the absolute minimum. When the command 'Torpedo away!' was given, the boat would surface, and its distance from the target ship could be measured. One approach followed another – and then there followed the night shooting.

Basically it was all quite a cheerful business. The group tried to put one over on me, and I had to stick to my guns. Conversations went something like this: 'The next attack will begin in a few minutes. Next letter in the alphabet is M. Meier into the tower for the next shot.' 'Did you hear that? I'm ordered up for the next shot . . .'. 'Gentlemen, if the one who's next on the list doesn't appear at once, I shall be obliged to take a hard line . . .'. 'Did you hear that? He's going to take a hard line . . .'. 'Even with you, Herr Meier. Joke over, gentlemen, the next attack is starting – into the tower with you!'.

Memel was just an interlude. It was winter, the thermometer fell and fell, and in East Germany more so than elsewhere. The sea was covered with ice floes; picking up the torpedoes afterwards became more and more difficult by the day. The course had to be abandoned. The journey back through the Baltic to Kiel took on the character of an expedition; the *Nordland* with its icebreaker bow-cap in front, followed by the two little 'canoes', and finally the catcher ships, two old torpedo boats. The winter of 1940/41 was easily as cold as the previous year.

A few weeks before my twenty-fifth birthday new orders reached me. 'On the orders of the Supreme Commander you are to take command of the *U-564*, currently in the final stages of completion. You will take command on 1 March 1941 and supervise the dockyard trials.' That was it! At last I had my own boat, a brand-new one too! The boat was in Hamburg at the yard of Blohm and Voss, the traditional birthplace of hundreds of merchant ships. It was a Type VIIC boat, weighed 750 tons, had two diesel engines producing 3,000HP between them, and two electric motors each of 750HP. It could cruise at 17 knots on the surface (though not half as fast when dived), could take fourteen torpedoes on board for a patrol and fire them from four torpedo tubes in the bow and one in the stern, etc, etc, etc . . . In a word, apart from a few small details, *U-564* was a replica of *U-48*, on which I had gone to sea nine times. I knew that boat by heart and could find my way around it blindfolded.

Its construction was supervised by my distinguished LI, Oberleutnant (Reserve) Gabler, in civilian life a ship-builder by profession, who had prior to that been involved with designing submarines in Holland. He was a quite remarkable man, and a real expert, and ensured that the crew were acquainted with the features and workings of the boat. I put in an appearance from time to time so that the crew could get to know me. Between times I went ashore to acquaint myself with Hamburg, where I put up in a hotel in St Pauli. Despite the usual wartime blackout, the lack of foreign traffic and the temporary absence of the usual Hanseatic glamour, Hamburg still continued to cast a certain spell over a visitor. After all the struggles and privations I was able to take things easy and get my breath back. Here I could meet up in pretty splendid settings with friends and mates from the various dockyards, as well as making a professional job of supervising my boat being commissioned. It was quite by chance that I noticed, one fine day or early evening, that I was being shadowed by two men. And it wasn't just on a single occasion but repeatedly. Indeed, so as to make things easier for them I often gave them a hand, saying loudly to my friends, 'Come on, let's go to the Bronzekeller' – or the Roxybar, or whatever was the case, only to find their by now well-known faces surfacing there too. And that was how one day I came to be ordered to present myself to Admiral von Friedeburg. He had a comprehensive dossier – four typewritten pages – from the Abwehr in front of him, that was intended to shoot me down in flames. 'Among other things in there, it states that Suhren sits at the bar in uniform

The officers and crew of *U-564* parade formally on deck for the commissioning of the boat.

with a black man' . . . 'Sure, Herr Admiral, there was an African in a bar; he often sat there. I didn't think anything of it; I assume he came from the colonies'. 'Suhren pays his bill with a suspect cheque from Ahlmanns, a Jewish bank, and seems to feel no shame about being seen in the most superior places with a Jewish girl . . .'. 'Sure, Herr Admiral,' I replied, 'If all German girls were as blond and blue-eyed and sweet-looking as they're supposed to be, we'd have nothing to complain about. I didn't feel there was any problem attached to going out with this girl. She's nice. I got to know her at a Craft Fair. Her elder sister has been engaged for a year and a day to our staff-doctor on the destroyer *Max Schultz*, and he's having difficulties with his marriage-permit; in fact he hasn't got one yet. It's quite true that the girl isn't completely Aryan. What of it?' 'Suhren is celebrating the commissioning of his boat at the hotel of Frau Bauernfeind, of all people, whose sister recently fled to South America via Spain and Portugal'. 'What is 'fled' supposed to mean? She has a residence in South America and in fact has citizenship to go with it too.' Well, the allegations the Abwehr made in the document were incredible. 'So what . . .?' I kept saying, feeling confident that I'd done nothing wrong. Finally von Friedeburg fiddled a bit with the document, and then took his green pencil and noted, 'Complete rubbish' in the margin; which was enough to put me in the clear again. And that was the end of that.

As far as the regulations about Aryans and Jews were concerned, our time was spent in being chased around on the high seas, so we got little news of what was really going on at home. Two years later during a holiday I visited my parents, and travelled through Berlin. I noticed some old ladies and gentlemen in the Kurfurtstendamm wearing a yellow star on their clothing. Entirely naively, I asked one of the group I met what it meant. He looked at me in amazement. 'My dear sir, that is the Star of David which we are obliged to wear.' That was still running through my mind when I sat down in a street café. Two members of the Hitler Youth crossed over to me. They wanted my autograph, or something signing. I was pretty short with them, and refused. It wasn't the boys who were to blame, and they were surprised and offended. So had I been, but for quite a different reason.

In April 1941 I put *U-564* into service with all the formality of 'Upper deck, attention! Salute the flag!', and so on; for the first time I flew my narrow command pennant. I felt absolutely in my element. Just twenty-five years old, I was of the opinion that I had the best boat in the world under my feet, and did everything I could do to make it ready for the Front as quickly as possible. As usual we dealt in succession with the running-in of the engines, turning, and diving (aiming to vanish in less than 30 seconds); then gunnery and (even more important) torpedo-shooting were the order of the day. We practised all sorts of emergency procedures with the AGRU-front, and practised attack procedures on convoys by way of tactical training in the eastern Baltic. It was during one such practice attack on the battleship *Bismarck*, which was under way at the time, that I became conscious of the menacing turning of the propellers again, and was reminded of Norway, where in the same way the old *Warspite* had terrified the wits out of us. During the first weeks the visit of the 'GRÖFAZ' took place, 'The Greatest Commander of All Time', to whom my brother and I had been introduced on board the *Tirpitz*; I had little suspected that I was destined to cross his path again. We took part in an exercise in the deep Danish Bight, and as far north as the island of Bornholm, where we had a night off. We set foot in this quiet beauty spot and ate fried eggs just as though it were peacetime.

The time taken preparing for the Front varied from boat to boat, depending on the experience of the Kommandant, and more importantly on how well he could control his crew. By now, in the third year of the war, this process had slowed down noticeably, and it lasted as long as it had to. In my case I just needed to get the hang of the behaviour of the new boat. Otherwise there weren't any particular problems; I had already had practical experience of everything else. And my crew who numbered around fifty were not exactly dim either, so everything went off relatively quickly, and by June we could take our place in the Atlantic ready to go on to the next stage.

True, I did get a move on in the early stages, and demanded a lot of everyone. My 1WO, Oberleutnant zur See Fritz Mumm, wasn't entirely in agreement with it. 'What are you complaining about?', I asked him in a quiet moment in the mess. 'Don't you agree with me that during training I can't let anything – anything at all – slip by, whether it be in the handling of the boat or in matters of discipline? Didn't you serve on the *Graf Spee* before you were transferred to the Submarine service?' My No 1 nodded. 'Yes, but what's that got to do with it?' 'Didn't the Kommandant there always have the ship under his thumb – wasn't his reputation well-known? Wasn't he fully familiar with the qualities of his officers? And how does the Kommandant of such a large ship operate, with a crew of hun-

U-564 leaves port for an Atlantic patrol, Suhren on the bridge.

dreds? Moreover I have heard tell that there were specific orders about which ship or group of warships the battleship was allowed to launch an attack on; am I right? Yes?' My No 1 agreed. 'Something like that, even though I can't swear to it. But what's that got to do with us?'

'Let me explain', I continued. 'I expect you, the three officers and four junior officers, to be aware of what the crew can cope with, so that I can judge how far to push them. And as commander of a submarine, I am obliged to take on any and every enemy ship, unless I am specifically instructed not to. And as far as you are concerned, you were only a cog in the machine on the *Graf Spee*, hardly in a position to influence the course of the drama. But here, you are the No 1, and it is your duty to support me to the utmost of your ability, and to lead from the front if anything were to happen to me. I know very well what is in store for us out there; it will bring tears to your eyes. Every week, every day that we can get finished earlier and get to the Front is an advantage. For the submarine war is getting tougher and tougher. The sooner we get ourselves used to the dangers associated with it, the sooner we'll be able to cope with them and survive. Hence my very quick and intensive training. Our lives depend on getting every detail right.' He thought about it, and had to admit that I was right.

Sure, I wanted to know everything that went on, although at first sight that might seem to be at variance with my liberal nature. There was for example the matter of the bottle of rum in a basket on the first trip. Because of the lack of available space, we'd stowed provisions in every possible nook and cranny; the 10-litre bottle was placed in the ammunition store, on top of the shells. And it was supposed, of all things, to have got smashed in there by a shell being put back when we had to break off the fight with an escort. Anyway, on the way back home, when I wanted to 'splice the mainbrace', not a drop of the 10-litre bottle could be found. A blind man with a stick would have realised that things weren't as they should be – especially as the cook had once been reported to me as drunk, though I had been called to the bridge at the time and had forgotten the incident.

While provisions were being taken on board for the next patrol, and were stacked up on the pierhead waiting to be brought onto the boat, I made myself comfortable in the officers' wardroom with a beer and a scotch, where I could keep an eye on the ammunition store. Just as well I did. After a bit, the cook appeared, with a new bottle of rum, to stow it in the ammunition store again. I cleared my throat – 'Come on, cook; take the bottle back. No arguing, the rum is stopping ashore.' The cook obeyed my order reluctantly and went ashore again with the bottle. As soon as he'd gone, the provisioning officer on duty ashore appeared and planted himself in front of me. 'Now then, what's going on?' The radio operator who was in charge of provisions explained to me that according to the standard provisioning arrangements for submarines, 10 litres of rum were supposed to be on board to treat cases of hypothermia; that being the case, it was not permitted for me to . . . 'No, no. Look, Radio Operator, I'm not arguing with what you're saying. But it would be a shame for all that lovely rum to trickle out again into the ammunition store instead of down chilled throats. I often get pretty cold myself on the bridge – but I'm still overruling the provisioning schedule. I enjoy a drink ashore, but I never touch a drop on patrol. Do you have a problem with this?' After the indignant radio operator the LI appeared; he stuck his head round the door and asked innocently, 'Well, Herr Oberleutnant, have you found out yet who drank the rum?' I gave a grim laugh; 'Believe me, I'll get to the bottom of it. Nothing ought to happen on my boat that I don't know about.' The LI shoved off and left me to my third bottle of beer and the scotch.

In the meantime the bulk of the provisions were stowed on board under Obersteuermann Karl Limburg, who was in charge of the provisions on the boat. He was a good chap, and like all of similar rate was known among the officers by the friendly low-German nickname of 'Stürkorl'. I happened to notice that he kept creeping past me – rather too often. 'Obersteuermann, what's up?' That stopped him in his tracks. 'I should like to have a word with the Herr Oberleutnant'. 'Nothing's stopping you – sit down here and have a beer on me.' 'But Herr Oberleutnant, I'm still on duty . . .' 'Come on, surely you can put away just the one – after all, you've already been "having one on me" from the rum-bottle which was supposed to be broken on the last patrol. My bunk is immediately over the ammunition store, and I didn't smell a thing.' 'Tcha, tcha, I don't know anything about that, Herr Oberleutnant!' 'This is no laughing matter, Obersteuermann. You're the one in charge of provisions. Now then, out with it, what really happened?' Stürkorl shuffled uneasily this way and that. Apparently he was having difficulty getting his words out. 'Well, Herr Oberleutnant, how can I put it? Well, it's like this. You see, I'm forty years old now, and no longer exactly the youngest crewmember, and I have a problem with my circulation. I always need a little drop just to make sure I'm on top form. So the cook tapped off two bottles of rum for me at a time, until eventually there was none left. Of course I feel very badly about the whole thing now, especially since everyone is being made to suffer for it.'

So it was the one in charge of provisions who had taken the initiative himself; a case of the fox being set to guard the geese! And what to say about it? For a while I sat in silence. Karl Limburg was breathing heavily, and I was thinking. Then I looked at him. 'Good, Obersteuermann, now at last I know the answer. But tell me, doesn't that seem to you to be a breach of trust between us? I wonder why you didn't feel able to come to me and tell me exactly what the situation was. What have I done wrong?' Now he found it harder still, and lapsed back into the third person. 'The Herr Oberleutnant was so strict and inflexible during training that he had strictly forbidden us to take any private alcohol supplies on board; that is why I was reluctant to speak to the Herr Oberleutnant about it. Now, after we've done a patrol, the Herr Oberleutnant is quite a different person, much more friendly and approachable. And besides, I quite understand that all the hard training has been well worth it.'

'Now look here, Stürkorl.' It was pretty obvious before that the cook had been tapping off the bottle on the orders of a higher authority, so to speak. But I didn't want to land him in trouble; that would have smacked of informing or suchlike, and been bad for the relations with the crew on board. 'Well, you've admitted to me that you were taking the rum for medicinal purposes. In future, take enough alcohol on board for your circulation to survive the strain of a few weeks; then we won't need to have any more bottles broken in the ammunition store.' So the episode closed on a friendly note.

My boat *U-564* was part of the 1st Flotilla, which was stationed in the French naval port of Brest. From there we were able to set out for anywhere in the world and then creep back into the submarine bunkers whose 6m-thick concrete roofs were impregnable against any of the bombs of the time. Just once we ran up to Lorient, when our engines were completely worn out and needed to be changed.

The sea was mapped out and divided into squares, themselves sub-divided into smaller squares, which served as position-locators. The BdU's HQ at Kerneval kept continuously in touch with all the boats by radio and instructed them where to go. The idea was also to keep tabs on the weather in the Atlantic; the Kriegsmarine sent disguised fishing boats and even sailing boats to various places as 'weather-watchers'. One of the first orders we got banished *U-564* to some such weather station below Greenland, in a remote area where there weren't any ships to sink. Perhaps they wanted to test out the boat first before it got sent to a war zone. After I'd bobbed about up there pretty pointlessly for three weeks I lost interest in the job, and let the BdU know that there wasn't a lot doing up there. The reply promptly came back, 'Suhren to operate on the Gibraltar route.' So I had a fair distance to travel to get down there.

Mist and fog came in succession. With the visibility as bad as this we travelled mostly underwater, hoping to pick up propeller noise with our hydrophones. We had to keep diving and listening, then surfacing again and having a look round to see if the visibility had improved. This hanging about waiting was bad for the nerves. We couldn't do a thing. I lost patience with it, and had a signal sent; 'Visibility continuously bad for six days, request permission to move further south'. The reply to it was not encouraging; it simply said '*U-564* to maintain radio silence'. It puts a strain on morale on board, to have to keep getting through fuel and provisions without any prospect of achieving anything. For we need success in the same way as a performer needs applause. Without this sort of affirmation it would no longer be possible to overcome the occasional moments of terror.

Eventually, on the morning of the seventh day a reconnaissance Condor sights a convoy headed in the general direction of south – probably going towards Gibraltar. *U-564* along with other boats is immediately put onto it. Finally we are able to go into action again, and we steer a course of 161 degrees, at 15 knots. If all goes well, we should be able to make contact tomorrow around midday. I make sure the bridge watch is in a state of maximum alertness. I need seven hours of sleep in between times, though one never knows what will happen from one moment to another. Ewald, my radio-operator and de-coder, has orders not to allow anyone near my bunk. One shout from the bridge, and I spring onto my feet as though stung by a tarantula; but one can only sleep properly in pyjamas. And many's the time I've fallen onto the bridge in pyjamas, with my red scarf and binoculars round my neck.

I give orders to be called shortly before daybreak. I feel fresh and sufficiently rested to cope with the pursuit and the battle. The Gibraltar convoys are the most strongly defended, but carry the most important war-materials. According to the radio signals from the BdU, there are now eight boats taking part in the operation against the convoy. I stay on the bridge all day, so as not to miss any little puff of smoke or the tip of a mast-head, but it isn't till evening that we get a sighting report from Adalbert Schnee in *U-201*. Adi is pretty tenacious when it comes to keeping contact, so hopefully he'll stay with it and not let the convoy get away from him.

We are now 30 sea-miles behind the convoy, which is moving at 9 knots. We should catch up with it in five hours. Although Adi continues to report contact, we don't seem to be managing to get a glimpse of the convoy ourselves. Our own position may not be any too accurate, since we haven't shot a star-sight for eight days – only a noon sun. However precisely Stürkorl plots our course, that is, draws our course on the chart by dead-reckoning, he cannot make the necessary allowances for the currents. *U-204* (Walter Kell) and *U-559* (Hans Heidtmann) give progress reports. Two hours later Adi is ready to shoot.

I am glued to the binoculars. If we're anywhere near correct, we ought to be able to see the convoy sooner or later. But we arrive too late, contact has been lost. We get orders from the 2 i/c Naval Command to join a search line the next evening. The boats lie like a barrier diagonally across the Gibraltar route. We take up the most westerly position and see what comes our way . . .

. . . Suddenly we're onto a convoy. 'LI, keep the boat level at periscope depth' – exactly 14m. Five minutes later the starboard escort wanders past us. From the three rows of the convoy we latch on to the starboard column. Up periscope briefly, a quick look in the direction of the escort. Periscope down again, turned in the direction of the convoy and up again briefly.

All looks good. The sea is calm, so the boat is easy to hold at the right depth. Periscope up one more time in the direction of the convoy. Damn, what's going on? They're all tacking to starboard. Periscope down, move back. Things have suddenly become tricky; we're sitting right in the middle of them as they continue their turn. The middle column is coming just about straight at us. I can't get outside the convoy any more; so, nothing for it but to meet them head on. 'Grünert, no more than 10 degrees on the rudder. LI, keep the boat at exactly that depth'. Everything is said in a whisper. The leading freighter is already only 500m off. Between the rows of ships there is a distance of only about 400m. I shall only be able to turn towards the starboard column at the last minute, otherwise I shan't have room.

The periscope goes up in the meantime, just for a second so as not to give ourselves away. All five torpedoes are made ready to shoot. The front freighter of the column pushes on, now only 15m away, just beside me, high as a house and near enough to touch. It nearly runs us down. In front of me in the starboard column I've spotted a worthwhile target – a tanker.

'Bosun, what speed are we doing?' 'A good 10 knots, Herr Oberleutnant. Bearing left 30 degrees, bearing changing'. 'Grünert, report state of readiness, please!' 'Tubes 1 and 2 ready'. 'Bosun, let me know when we have bearing 60 degrees.' The words fall like drops.

The bosun reports 'Bearing 50 degrees'. 'Grünert, rudder amidships'. 'Bearing 60 degrees – now!' 'Tube 1 – ready! Tube 1 – fire! Hard to port, course 120 degrees'. We run parallel with the convoy. An explosion rings out; the tanker is hit! A quick glance round. Further astern two more tankers are turning immediately away from each other, one south, the other north. 'Tube 5 – ready! Tube . . . What's going on? I can't see a thing'. LI confirms, 'Boat level at 14m'. My God! We are completely enveloped in a thick cloud of black smoke. The tanker's burning like a torch and the smoke is covering everything in a dark cloud. I cannot see anything, and decide with a heavy heart to dive deep. The situation is tricky. We're directly below the convoy, just on the next floor down. No one could guess we're here, and there's no chance of depth-charges in this position; but there is a considerable risk of being rammed.

The propeller noise gets quieter and quieter and vanishes into the distance. Nothing can be heard of the fast escort vessels; it could be that one is hanging around quietly waiting for us. We go to periscope depth again; still nothing more to be seen. But its getting pretty smoky, and after we've surfaced visibility is down to about 3,000m. It's an awkward situation for our boat to be in. If a destroyer were to creep up on us out of the gloom, we'd have a job getting away, and there would be always the chance of getting caught by gunfire. I decide to turn off to the south.

The convoys didn't follow an absolutely consistent course, but tacked on command because of the danger from submarines, so as to make themselves more difficult targets in the event of an attack. Their routes across the ocean lay principally in two directions. One of them ran from North America or Canada to Great Britain and back. They would be accompanied by escorts from each end, which would meet in the middle of the Atlantic and switch over to the one going in the opposite direction. (The route to Murmansk, supplying the Russians, didn't yet exist.) The other route the convoys travelled on was the Gibraltar route, nearer the coast, which ran to and from various points far away. Ships came singly, for instance, round the Cape of Good Hope, formed a convoy off Freetown/West Africa, and at the top off Gibraltar continued

Suhren and Mützelburg ashore.

in company with ships from the Mediterranean, or they split up and went in opposite directions. Because the coasts with their air-bases were so near these convoys were heavily defended from the air.

The same could not be said of the American convoys. The range of aircraft was at that time relatively limited, so in the middle of the North Atlantic there was a so-called quiet zone, where no enemy planes could reach us. It was known as the 'Gap'. This 'strip' or 'chink' became smaller and smaller as the war progressed and in the end closed up completely. But at that stage they were comparatively peaceful waters, where all we had to do was keep an eye on the horizon and relax.

And here one fine day I met *U-203*, under Kapitänleutnant Rolf Mützelburg, who had served alongside me from the beginning of the submarine campaign. The crew were dug out of their holes and enjoyed the lovely weather and the warm sunshine. They messed around in their swimming trunks like children let out to play, Mützelburg always well to the fore. They were playing tag when Mützelburg ran up the conning tower and dived in elegantly headfirst off the top of the bridge into the water. My hair stood on end, and I said to him, 'What did you do that for? You wouldn't catch me doing that. It's reckless; the boat is so narrow that with its fuel tanks bulging out on the side it's not that easy to dive across them.' But he laughed, and told me he did it quite often, and had no intention of stopping. Then he continued on his way. Three days later a radio-report reached me. Mützelburg had dived in yet again, this time from his own bridge, but had missed the water and had cracked his skull on the side-tank. Shortly afterwards he was dead. And that was how one of the most successful submarine commanders lost his life.

7

Oak Leaves and Kapitänleutnant – Schnapps with Hitler – Across the pond – Scheherezade: cherchez la femme!

I DID SIX PATROLS WITH *U-564*, in the course of which I sank about thirty-three ships. I shall explain in a moment why I add 'about'. To give a full account of the attack on each ship would take too long. When one spells them out they are often very similar, so I am going to content myself with a 'fast-forward', and only go into details occasionally. It was no longer possible to achieve the quick successes of the first year of the war. The situation had got much more difficult, and much more risk was involved. That was especially true of the Gibraltar route, where the planes kept us down and tried to separate us from the convoys; before we could surface again the convoy was up and away.

Of the thirty-three ships mentioned, twenty-three were identified with certainty. The British corvette *Zinnia*, which was blown sky-high: the American tanker *Eclipse*, which sank in the shallow waters of the Straits of Florida with its funnels sticking out, round which we had to make a wide berth: the Canadian tanker *Victolite*, the *Empire Oak*, the *Potrero del Llano*, to name but a few. We shot from outside the convoy and off to the side; the convoy travelled in rows, or 'columns', and in fact if one could just get a shot in one could always hit one of them as it came into the line of fire, or at least hit the next one beyond it. We didn't actually see many of the hits, we simply heard them. It went down in the log as, for example: '. . . Heard 4 separate explosions, saw three separate bursts of flame, followed by lifeboats'; '*U-564* heard 4 explosions between 1min.15secs and 1min.27secs, so presumably got two hits each on the *Lavington Court* and an unknown ship as well'; '. . . heard 5 explosions after firing 5 torpedoes, observed 2 bursts of flame and a high plume of smoke . . .'. And finally the failures need to be mentioned as well; like '. . . after 59 and 79 seconds *U-564* heard the impact of the torpedoes, but no explosions: presumably failed to detonate.'

A word too about the business of 'tonnage sunk'. That was the only yardstick according to which the BdU awarded praise and decorations. At the end of the day he needed something to latch on to. For a start, my twenty-three ships sunk and identified by name, amounted to 125,000 tons according to the International Register of Shipping; the unknown ten raised the level to about 200,000 tons. Quoting only tonnage and comparing figures sounds pretty lame; how it was achieved is much more important.

I was a specialist in attacking convoys; a difficult job. Every time a convoy went to Gibraltar and I was anywhere near, I was put on the job. And in spite of extensive sea and air protection it was often a matter of pretty small ships, former coasters weighing only between 1,000 and 1,500 tons. These barely made worthwhile targets, and were difficult to hit as well. Colleagues who had been there previously claimed to have sunk tankers of '6,000 or more tons . . .'. I hardly saw one tanker on the Gibraltar run. There certainly were on the North Atlantic run, but here – scarcely at all. But better to say nothing and not land anyone in the soup! Moreover the British never released figures of ships lost. And it's especially difficult to judge a ship's size at night – one could be running shoulder to shoulder with it, as did indeed happen. As already mentioned, I was often unable to observe the sinking of a ship or to judge exactly how big it was due to the heavy enemy counter-attack. When things got back to normal again, there was no sign of anybody and we were up and away ourselves.

Dönitz said to me once at the end of a pep-talk, 'Exactly how many ships do you think you have sunk now?' 'Well, goodness, it must be about sixteen this year. But I can't say with any certainty that they were always completely sunk .' 'Yes, well, how high would you put your tonnage then?' 'That is hard to be sure about as well, Herr Admiral'. Dönitz turned to his staff: 'Yes, but what are we to do, then, when some see the ships as big, and some as small, and they can't be sure they've really sunk them? I've got an idea. We'll give Suhren 5 points for each hit with a torpedo, whether it sank a ship or not. That makes 80 points for a start. In addition, he's sunk a warship, a corvette, for which he gets 10 points, making 90 points altogether. And for good leadership he gets another 2 points each time, which makes a grand total of 100.' And he finished his deliberations by saying, 'So, we ought to do something for Suhren. Whenever he's onto a convoy, I can go to sleep peacefully at night and know that he'll stay with it.' And that was how it came about that I was also allowed to include in my total those considerable tonnages of shipping in the sinking of which I had 'taken the leading role'.

At the end of 1941, I and my boat were laid up in dock, very much the worse for wear from bomb damage. On New Year's Eve I was to be awarded the Oak Leaves to my Knight's Cross, a decoration that had at that time only been awarded to a handful of submariners. Heinrich Lehmann-Willenbrock of *U-96* and Kapitän zur See Rogge of the auxiliary cruiser *Atlantis* were to be given the same award. We were all summoned to the Wolfsschanze, the 'Wolf's Lair' to be decorated. The 'Wolf's Lair' was the Führer's Operational Headquarters, a extensive and well-camouflaged bunker complex in the thick woods of East Prussia, near Rastenburg.

After reporting to Naval Command in Berlin, the three of us travelled by train to East Prussia. When we reached our destination, we were welcomed by Hitler's naval adjutant, Kapitän zur See von Puttkamer, who led us to the Führer's bunker and invited us to tea after the ceremony. That was when I heard,

Hitler decorates Suhren with the 'Eichenlaub', the Oak Leaves; beyond him Lehmann-Willenbrock and Rogge.

confidentially, that at the end of the year the Russians had broken through the centre of the German line, and Hitler had only managed to stem the German retreat by issuing very strict orders. I was dying to enquire whether there were any political alternatives to continuing the war, since in the long term things looked pretty bleak for the submarine campaign as well; so I tried to steer the conversation cautiously in that direction.

But Kapitän Rogge, who had spent a year and a half sitting on his cruiser, talked and talked. 'Mein Führer, here are some photos . . . and some more . . . and in this one . . .'; and every time I thought Hitler was about to start on one of his endless monologues (of which I'd already had a taste on the *Tirpitz*), Rogge interrupted again with his photos. I can quite understand Rogge's behaviour; after a year and a half at sea on his own he just wanted to get things off his chest. And it was probably just as well; who knows how Hitler would have reacted to my impertinent questions?

Rogge's ship, the raider *Atlantis.*

Dinner that evening, at which Hitler was usually present at that stage of the war, brought us all together again. Despite being a junior Oberleutnant I sat next to Generalfeldmarschall Keitel, Supreme Head of the Armed Forces, who was later to be hung by the Allies. Opposite me sat General Dietl of the Mountain Troops, one of the most charismatic generals of the war years. Rogge sat next to Hitler. At the end of the meal everyone was given a schnapps. At that time in the Führer's HQ they had – to my delight – naval schnapps glasses, holding the best part of half a litre. Hitler was teetotal, and nodded to Keitel, who proposed the toast. Off we launched, with arms raised to the second button and bows in all directions, 'Your very good health!' etc etc. The others took formal and decorous sips, but I tipped the glass up in my usual way and downed it in one. It was all gone; amazement on all sides. Hitler laughed, looked at the adjutant and gave him a signal with his hand, and immediately he came across and I got a second one, full to the brim. Well, I thought that since I could obviously get a decent glass of schnapps there, I might as well polish that one off too. I'm not one for dainty manners; I'm only a simple seaman, and they'd better get used to it. Hitler himself seemed to like these sort of spontaneous gestures, which he could see were free of the usual sort of toadying and grovelling.

Dietl was impressive. He said in his Bavarian dialect – 'I'm an amphibian; I have the dagger of the Navy and of the Air Force, and I've been decorated by all three branches of the

Services, all for Narvik.' Somehow or other, though, he seemed nervous, as though he was waiting for something. He kept on asking, 'The Head of the SS is coming, isn't he?' And he was told, 'Yes, yes, he's definitely coming.' And then Heinrich Himmler actually appeared, looking not at all like the sparkling Germanic hero of his Racial Philosophy: distinctly unprepossessing, with spectacles and close-cropped hair, and a marked contrast in appearance to the weather-beaten general from the mountains. I pricked up my ears and took a seat near them, so that I could eavesdrop and discover what Dietl was so worried about. And I heard him begging Himmler; 'Reichsführer, could you possibly let me have 1,500 of your leather coats for my troops? They're sat there quietly freezing to death, because they haven't got any proper winter kit.' Clearly it must have been up to Himmler himself to give instructions about the leather coats, which were lying around somewhere in SS stores, and Dietl had to go on his knees for his mountain troops. Himmler gave permission, anyway. 'Yes, sure, of course you can have them'. That episode made a marked impression on me. Up to that time I had always been under the impression that everything in the Third Reich was arranged and organised in the best possible way. From that moment on I became more sceptical; and I remembered the warning my father had given me.

From the Wolf's Lair we went back to Berlin to report to Großadmiral Raeder. Raeder had invited us to breakfast at 14.00 in the Kaiserhof with the members of the Admiralty. Lehmann-Willenbrock and I had only just finished bending the elbow – as one might expect! – in the early hours of the morning. Raeder was always trying to steer clear of my influence, just in case . . . Anyway, when your heart is full, your mouth overflows, as we say. My mouth didn't exactly overflow, but in the course of our conversation, I did let slip a remark that I would gladly have taken back afterwards. When Raeder came to the matter of the torpedoes, he asked, 'What do you make of it then, Suhren?' I answered pretty accurately, 'Herr

Admiral, they are rotten, but of course quite a few would have missed anyway.' So Raeder turned to Dönitz, saying 'One of your best Kommandants says that a lot would have missed, but you're telling me the torpedoes are to blame.' Naturally the truth lay somewhere in the middle. But that wretched Suhren had put his foot in it once again.

After the meal Raeder said goodbye and took himself off on his own. Before the admirals dispersed, I commented, 'There seems to be quite a stockpile of surplus alcohol next door; might I take it upon myself to invite you to a drink?' These admirals were all good chaps, who basically envied us young officers; for in order to become a leader of the fleet and be a cut above the rest of us, they had had to give up their commands. There were now only a very few big ships: *Tirpitz*, *Scharnhorst* and *Gneisenau* for the younger ones, and perhaps the *Hipper* and the *Lützow*. There could be only one Admiral of the Fleet, Admiral Lütjens, and he was already no friend of mine what with the *Bismarck* and the destroyer flotilla.

But on this occasion they celebrated our success. As we were enjoying ourselves, one of them asked, I don't remember who, 'Tell me, Suhren, which Crew do you actually belong to?' 'Ah well,' I answered, 'we'd better not talk about that. I'm way behind now, and I'll be the last in line for promotion.' (I thought of my unjust treatment at the Naval Academy, and how my past record still continued to hold me back.) But then came the question, 'How's that happened, and why? The Luftwaffe can make accelerated promotions so why can't we? It's ridiculous that you're wearing the Oak Leaves and are still only an Oberleutnant. Look, Schulte-Mönting, why don't you suggest to the Großadmiral that we make Suhren a Kapitänleutnant?' 'Yes', he replied, 'good idea!'

In my state of general euphoria, all that went in at one ear and out of the other. But the next day I was back with Großadmiral Raeder to receive the submarine badge with Diamonds to the Oak Leaves. Suddenly Raeder exclaimed,

'Suhren, in recognition of your service, I promote you herewith to Kapitänleutnant'. Admiral Schulte-Mönting was standing behind Uncle Erich, and smiled. I must have looked completely dumbfounded, for Raeder asked, 'What's up with you, Suhren? Don't you believe that I can . . .?' So, the next day after getting the Oak Leaves I became Kapitänleutnant, on 1 January 1942.

As he left, Raeder told me that I would have to come back the next day to see him again; the submarine badge with diamonds was made to a special design, and wasn't ready yet. I replied, 'Großadmiral, there's a small problem. My boat is finally ready for sea after a month of repairs. I can't keep them hanging about for another day'. Then the Highest of All said, 'But suppose I put my plane at your disposal, that would save you a day. Does that solve the problem?' 'Yes, Großadmiral, that's fine!' So I flew from Berlin to Lorient with a courier, all on my own. That was an unheard of privilege. I was still so full of booze, that even the stern Raeder was amused – and that's saying something!

The next patrol took me a long way off with *U-564*, right away from my former stamping-ground to the East Coast of America. Germany and Italy had declared war on the USA in December 1941. This had legalised the position that had more or less existed for a while, as a consequence of America helping Great Britain by supplying war-materials, of undisguised threats to the Axis powers, and of armed incidents at sea. Still, America seemed about as far off as the Moon, between 3,000 and 4,000 nautical miles away. In order to mount an attack over there where it was least expected – namely on their very doorstep – it needed a long arm, and our old submarine types couldn't manage it without extra help. We were worried about finding room for the necessary quantities of oil and provisions in the limited space we had available. Nevertheless on 13 January 1942 came the beginning of a series of attacks which became known as 'Operation Drumbeat'.

From an exchange of blows at a distance it soon developed

into close combat, reaching all the way along the busy American coastal route, from the St Lawrence to the Caribbean. We had enormous success. In the month of January alone, only a handful of submarines were responsible for sinking some sixty-two ships. The submarines could be counted on the fingers of two hands. Among the Kommandants were, for instance, Hardegen, Topp and Zapp, all 'beating their drum'. The distinguished Hardegen had the bright idea of reporting his successes in verse; Dönitz was not impressed at all. When I heard the radio-report go out in rhyme, I just thought – 'Oh dear, oh dear, oh dear, you've really put your foot in it now . . .', for the 'Lion' absolutely hated anything like that. The expected thunderstorm held off, though it rumbled on without making too much fuss. Such temptations are better resisted.

I first crossed the pond with the second wave. The LI had filled every available crevice – indeed just about every toothmug – with diesel oil. Travelling at our most economical speed so as to use as little fuel as possible we finally made it up to near Cape Hatteras, where we were convinced that the shipping was just waiting for us. Cape Hatteras was a favourite focal point for coastal shipping. However, it turned out rather differently.

I started by managing to sink the Canadian tanker *Victolite*, a juicy morsel of 11,500 tons. But then, just off the Cape, the crew reported to me on 13 February, 'German submarine approaching!' It turned out to be *U-106*, under the command of my old crewmate Harald Gelhaus. Visibility wasn't good. Dusk had already set in and the warm waters of the Gulf were giving off a mist in the wintry air. I had just had a nap, and was still rubbing my eyes, when the boat appeared through the gloom. It was hard to estimate its distance away from us and on this occasion I was way out in my reckoning. The 1WO alerted us at the last minute to the need to turn hard away from her, but it was too late. Despite 'full speed astern' the boat didn't stop in time. There was the noise of a dreadful crash, and when I looked at the damage, I had managed to slice into my friend Gelhaus' fuel tank. Gelhaus of course swore good and proper, since he now had to turn back and wouldn't be able to carry on. I had good reason to curse myself, too, and would happily have jumped overboard, for in the collision I had bent the doors of all four torpedo tubes, and would no longer be able to fire them. I also had to pump a few tons of fuel across to Gelhaus for his return journey. Despite being able to sink the British tanker *Opelia* (6,000 tons) by gunfire three days later, the whole expedition had nevertheless been a waste of time. When I reported back, it must have been obvious that I was unusually meek. Dönitz just looked down at me and said, 'You mutton-head!'

Subsequently I did manage to make up for the accident off Cape Hatteras; in just two weeks I managed to sink six ships (40,000 tons in all), in the Straits of Florida, that hundred miles of seaway between Florida and the Bahamas linking the Gulf of Mexico with the Atlantic. It is one of the most travelled sea lanes in the world. Even by January our submarines

Damage to the bows of *U-564* as a result of its collision with *U-106*.

had started making a nuisance of themselves out there. However, the beaches were still blazing with lights, business was going on as usual, and lighthouses and buoys twinkled away as though in peace time. It took a long time for the Americans, who had been taken completely by surprise, to grasp what was really going on here; it was a while before they declared the route to be a significantly dangerous war zone and strengthened their defences, which at first had been pretty feeble. It was only after six months, to be exact on 15 May 1942, that the Straits of Florida were finally completely blacked out.

In order to be able to continue our patrol for longer, *U-564* was refuelled while still at sea by one of the so-called 'Milch Cows'. These were particularly large submarines, intended simply to be used as mobile tankers. We met up with them in the Atlantic. It was the beginning of May. Another boat had put out a signal, 'Entry to Florida Straits impossible due to strong defence cover.' After such a long trek any number of such well-intended warnings weren't going to hold me back, so I soon experienced this 'strong defence'. I covered the whole length of the Florida Straits from North to South, sometimes off the Bahamas, sometimes off the American coast. By night we surfaced, and always left a glittering wake behind us in the phosphorescent Gulf Stream. That was inconvenient for us, since we tended to get planes flying over us none too high. I stopped the boat each time, not knowing whether they'd seen us or not, or indeed whether they would drop any bombs on us. They must have picked us up on their radar, but were probably in doubt as to whether we were one of their own patrol boats or just another small ship. Sometimes they used their searchlights as well, and that could indeed be touch and go.

We needed also to look out for the fast little Coast Guard patrol boats, which covered the straits armed with deck guns and depth-charges. We called them 'Ford gunboats' because they were supposed to have been produced in a hurry by Ford

Motors. On one occasion, up and across from Miami, I was uncertain as to how to deal with one, whether to go down to periscope depth or to dive deep, and got severely depth-charged at 50m as a reward for my indecision. Though the charges didn't hit us directly, they did all sorts of damage inside the boat itself. What was worst was that I was certain that this had had a bad effect on the torpedoes in the tubes. As a result of being so badly jarred, either the pistols (the detonation mechanism) had packed up, or the sensitive lateral and vertical steering controls were badly affected. On every occasion after serious depth-charge attacks, either we couldn't get our torpedoes to run properly or they failed to detonate.

Three Victory-type freighters crossed my path off Key West, the most southerly tip of the USA. They were empty, decked out in fresh paint and sailing along in line astern. They had obviously dropped straight off the branch – that is to say, they were fresh from the dockyard. I set the torpedoes at 3m, so as not to miss them by going underneath, and took careful aim at them from the relatively close range of 1,200m – and nothing happened, absolutely nothing! I heard the torpedoes hit below the waterline, and through the periscope saw people on the upper deck looking over the side: but nothing more than that. And they would all have made tasty morsels. Each one of the Liberty ships coming off the assembly line weighed 6,000 tons, and could carry 10,000 tons of cargo; and each Victory ship was 8,000 tons and could carry even more. All the same, I got my 40,000 tons including the tanker *Eclipse*; when she caught fire and sank she alarmed the whole of the Straits of Florida.

After our return, all these matters came up in our report to Dönitz at HQ: the improved technology of the enemy's defence, whose planes already seemed able to locate us by radar: their increased flying range, which was beginning to close the 'gap': the carrying of searchlights: and the new and effective depth-charges devised for carrying on board planes. There was also the matter of the security of our coded radio messages.

The tanker *Eclipse* down by the stern after being torpedoed by *U-564* off Boca Raton, Florida, 5 May 1942. (US National Archives)

During the trip to Florida we already had in use a code-machine (the 'Enigma') that was fitted with four rotors. It was superior to the previous three-rotor version, and caused the Allies a complete black-out for at least six months; in other words it made it impossible for them to read the coded messages which were exchanged between submarine command and the submarines themselves. We couldn't be sure, however, and therefore remained sceptical. As a colleague recounted to me, Kapitän zur See Rogge was extremely grateful for the rescue of his crew after the total destruction of his auxiliary cruiser. (Submarines had picked up the crew of his ship after it sank.) In the course of conversation with the BdU, Rogge let slip the suggestion that our code might not be watertight. Dönitz reacted very strongly to this suggestion; 'It's absolutely impossible, so it can't have happened'. That may or may not have been the case. A commanding officer always needs to prevent rumours like this spreading; the consequences would have been incalculable. I can understand his anger that this concern had even been voiced. In any case we already had the

Another victim of *U-564*: the tanker *Portrero del Llano* ablaze off Miami, 14 May 1942. (US National Archives)

Pati Behrs (later a film-star in the US) with Suhren and others at the Scheherezade Club in Paris.

fourth rotor arm, and the code had been made watertight again for a long time.

After reporting to Dönitz we went to the Scheherezade. It's a mystery why certain places hold a special fascination for certain types of people. Is it the surroundings, the atmosphere, the music, the luck of the draw, or perhaps a combination of all of these? The Scheherezade was a high-class bar somewhere in Paris. It was the meeting-place, indeed the regular haunt, of submarine officers. Even Dönitz himself wasn't shy about calling in there once in a while. Bleichrodt had brought me there in the first place. The Scheherezade was a breath of fresh air after a patrol, and was popular with people in general, in particular with single men back on home ground again. There was always a hearty welcome for one there: 'Hullo! The submarines are in again!' Every so often, though, one could see tears in the eyes of the young women who felt, with a woman's intuition, that 'their' submarine hadn't come back. They would sidle up hesitantly: 'Have you heard anything of Bertel?' There was nothing for it but to avoid the issue with something vague like, ' Oh, he'll be along soon, *certainement*, I'm sure he'll be back . . .' and so on, though we knew that it was four weeks since anyone had heard from him. Four weeks of radio silence was taken to mean a death-sentence. There could still be a faint hope that the English might release names of survivors; but that sometimes took its time, and it meant a long while of torment and uncertainty. I remember the blonde Natasha with her shoulder-length hair, Monique, a girl-singer as pretty as she was intelligent – and Pati. Pati married an American war-correspondent after France was liberated by the Allies. He left her in the lurch with two children, divorced her, and married a famous German film-actress.

France was cheap, and our pay was ample, augmented as is usual in all navies by a 'submarine allowance'. But everything got spent; it was as if we were saying, 'Hurrah! We're alive! Who knows what lies in store for us tomorrow?' One day I came into Headquarters, and Dönitz asked, 'Now then,

Suhren, what's up?' 'I'm fine, Herr Admiral, it's just that I've blown my pay.' 'Haven't you got anything left at all?' 'No, Herr Admiral, it's all completely gone.' So he turned to his adjutant: 'Fuhrmann, will you please get 400 marks from my private purse and let Suhren have it, so that he's got some money in his pocket for travel expenses?' I went easy on that money, and travelled to Dresden to spend my leave with my parents.

8

On the track of the enemy – The fourth night – The diesel-fire – Battle formation in the periscope!

SUMMER 1942. WE HAD JUST crossed the Bay of Biscay, and were steering a course westwards. U-boat Command had given me a free hand and had agreed to my filling-up in the Atlantic from a 'Milch Cow'. A comparatively quiet crossing lay ahead of us. Suddenly, however, as so often in time of war, it was a case of 'as you were'! A reconnaissance plane reported a convoy headed south. Since we were in the area at the time, we were inevitably drawn into the hunt. According to the position we had been given for it, we were due to make contact in three hours, or so my navigating officer calculated.

I'm back on the bridge again. With a calm sea and good visibility *U-564* is cruising at 15 knots in what we take to be the direction of the enemy. After three or four hours, there is still no sign of them; the position as reported by air-reconnaissance proves once again to be unreliable. For the moment we can only see what happens. We stick to our course, but continue at 12 knots.

When the watch is relieved, I have already been on my feet for five hours. In an hour it will begin to grow dark. Ahead of us the horizon is as sharp as an etching. Twenty minutes later, on the starboard bow, mastheads show up. The convoy! Off with a contact report, 'Quadrant XYZ'. Scarcely has the radio-signal been sent than the look-out is already shouting 'Plane!' We are well aware that there are three other submarines in our patrol, and the old familiar song rings out again – 'Alarm!'.

Loading *U-564* with stores before leaving for the Caribbean.

'Dive! Dive!' The plane must have seen us already. Tank 5 is beginning to hiss with escaping air as I jump down below. Being last, I close the hatch behind me. We glide down into the depths at a steep angle. At around 60m I give orders to level out. The depth-charges are sure to rain down on us now, and it's always important to have the boat on an even keel when they go off. All is well; the LI has the boat well under control, as ever. And no sign of any depth-charges. So, cautiously back up again; 20 metres, 16, 14, the boat is at periscope-depth. A quick look-round; the plane has vanished. Surface! Look round with the naked eye. Nothing to see – but no sign of the convoy either, the tips of whose mastheads we had seen just now. The sea has swallowed them up again. If my eyes don't deceive me, not a trace of a single one. Why can't I see anything? Damn! There's an escort-plane, coming straight at us. Alarm! Dive down to 100m – same again. Ask the listening-room, 'Can you hear anything?' 'Yes, the sound is getting louder.' Something is approaching on the surface. I alter course to 060, and steer off at an angle. The propeller noise travels past us, the volume fades out, leaving no sound for position-finding any more. I wonder whether the plane actually saw us, whether we were spotted by the patrol, or whether it is just circling continuously round the convoy to force U-boats underwater from the outset.

'LI, up to periscope depth', again. Up and down the whole time: it's like being in a lift! These fiendish air-patrols of the Allies. LI to Captain: 'Boat rising, 50 metres, 40, 30, 20, 15.' Periscope up, only for a few seconds. Nothing to be seen. The same thing repeated, this time slowly. Up above it is getting dark, night is beginning. '1st and 2nd officers of the watch to the Captain! Listen in – when we surface now, we'll split up the four sectors between us – and keep your eyes open, "wooden-eye"; stay on the alert!'

U-564 breaks the surface. In a moment we are up. Around us all seems clear. 'Blow tanks, full ahead both diesels, course 126, set up the watch on the bridge'. I grab the binoculars. The night is really dark, but the horizon is clearly visible. Thirty minutes pass. I ask the navigating officer, 'Where's the convoy?' We calculate it should be three nautical miles ahead of us. But there's nothing doing. It's vanished without a trace. The other boats have made no contact either. Radio-signal from U-boat Command; 'Form a search-line from quadrant X to quadrant Y, in a line moving north to south, covering 10 nautical miles. Maintain your positions in the search-line until 08.00 tomorrow'.

We have the westernmost position. I decide to steer at full speed ahead first southeast and then southwest, hoping to cross the course of the convoy. The WOs clear off, the Navigating Officer immerses himself in his work on the chart, I continue to stay on the bridge. So we reach our allotted sector precisely. But it is completely empty; no sign of any shipping. I don't like the search-line, and I send off a signal accordingly. 'Convoy presumed southeast of my position'. An evasive response from U-boat command; 'Maintain search-line; by 16.00 tomorrow another position to be reached'; new data given. 'Full ahead, and steer course 154'.

After another hour and a half the WO spots another plane – a Sunderland, which is a typical convoy escort. Surely the ships must soon be there. In the meantime it is past midnight, and the tension among the watch on the bridge reaches its peak. We gaze intently at the horizon over which anything may appear at any moment. 'Do you see what I'm seeing? A cloud of smoke, a cloud of smoke!' First barely visible, then gradually it gets denser. At last – it's the convoy. 'Navigating Officer, enemy bearing 150 degrees, distance about 15 miles. Look up which quadrant we're in; the radio-operator needs to give a contact-report.' And now begins the chase that we've been looking forward to. *U-564* stands well back. No more can be done during the hours of daylight, but by night we can get on with the job. The engines are running flat-out. The sea is reasonably calm, sea-state 3. There's a plane again already! Down goes the lift, one floor; watch the approaching plane through the sky-periscope. It rolls over to starboard and vanishes again. Surface!

Twice more the planes come over and we dive. It begins to grow darker; we have the convoy diagonally across from us. We

A U-boat on the surface was always a sitting target.

approach cautiously, making sure that whatever happens we don't lose sight of it again. However, we're not far enough ahead of it to be able to launch a successful attack. The freighters are still some three or four miles from us. Through the glasses the escorts can be clearly made out, two leading the convoy, and two more on our side of it. Another 1,000m, and I could get in four well-placed shots. But at the last minute, one of the escorts seems to smell us, comes flat out in our direction and threatens to force us down. Damn the tub! We show him our stern.

However, we don't lose contact again. Even before we're compelled to dive, the escort turns back to rejoin the convoy, and we can move in yet closer. The whole sequence repeats itself two or three times. It's two steps forward, one step back; just before we have a chance to shoot, everything goes wrong each time. It's a game of patience that needs nerves, as each turn of events sets us back again.

In the east it is beginning to turn grey. A new day is dawning across the water. We set a course to the west of the convoy against the dark horizon, so that we can see without being seen. I have been on the bridge right through the night. The extreme tension prevents one from feeling tired; only my back is aching as always from standing so long. It's a price one has to pay. A clear, calm morning dawns. And as the sun comes up, as the result of all these manoeuvres we have lost the convoy from sight again; our position is some 18 miles astern of it. The tips of the mastheads have long since vanished into thin air, instead of which periodically a puff of smoke appears. It happens more or less on a hourly basis. One of the ships is using coal in its boilers, and stokes them up every hour. It's a give-away signal for us, and one that the ship responsible is quite unaware of. I keep concentrating on the puffs of smoke, and warn the watch not to startle me by shouting. They are to point out any occurrences in good time – and quietly! My nerves aren't made of steel! I stay glued to the smoke cloud too, and don't dare close my eyes for a moment. Suddenly I hear the look-out on my right say – discreetly – 'Plane!' What's up? Are we spotted? A Sunderland whirrs through the air, a long way off. And the old game starts up again. 'Dive, LI; take the boat down to periscope-depth, please'. I've scarcely got focused on the plane when it's off again, and we surface after it has gone.

So it goes on all day, the third long day that we've been having fun shadowing this convoy. So as not to be spotted from the air, I keep away and out of sight of it, as least beyond the range normally covered by the escorting aircraft. That's around 25 nautical miles, and the aircraft comes round about every 45 minutes. Each time through diving we lose a quarter of an hour, which we need to make up afterwards. It's sickening. Shortly before dusk another German submarine appears. His course crosses ours from right to left. Via my bosun I send a message across. 'C(aptain) to C(aptain), I am in contact with the enemy. Steer on the same course as me, and don't get any closer to them.' 'Message received and understood.' I give more information: 'Convoy bears 60 degrees from me, about 20 miles away.' Ten minutes later I am travelling full ahead, course 090. If the other boat doesn't co-operate, the whole contact could be a waste of time. But he's in favour of working as a team, which is much as I expected. In half an hour we hope to have the freighters in full view ahead of us. Suddenly, once again, without any warning, 'Alarm!'– a plane comes up astern, shining a powerful searchlight on the water. As I leap down the hatch, I see the plane flying past my stern and catching the other boat in a cone of light. No more was seen or heard of the other boat after that. Whether it survived this particular encounter I don't know, but it remained unaccounted for.

It is the fourth night of our pursuit. We push on at full speed into the unknown, into the area where the darkening horizon is slightly blurred with shadows and smoke. Round about midnight we overtake the convoy, and steer northwards towards it. We close on them at our combined speed of around 25 knots. This is fast, and I must pull myself together, tired or not, for the next quarter of an hour will be the culmination of our chase which has gone on for three days and four nights.

My manoeuvre is unusual and a bit risky. On previous occasions, when I had gone in to attack from the usual shooting-angle of 45 degrees off to the side, I had often been spotted by the convoy escorts and forced down. This time I hope to take them by surprise them from dead ahead. The only problem is, how can I then get to the side out of the way of the convoy? The convoy steams on in three distinct columns. I have the middle one straight in front of me, and swing *U-564* across to the west. It is breathtaking to see how the shadows of the leading escorts float past without their becoming aware of us. We wait on tenterhooks. No one says a word. All one can hear is suppressed breathing. I pull the boat across the left even further. We are now between the outer column and the escorts alongside it, and therefore in the safety zone. I stop the diesel and keep an eye on the escort. He too changes course and swings out. Astern of him I swing the boat round to the right angle to fire from, but I'm too near the tall freighters. I need to be at least 400 or 500m away, so I go astern, a tricky movement for a U-boat captain in this situation! (What am I letting myself in for? Isn't the whole operation tricky enough already?)

Eight hundred metres away, the first freighter slides into my sights. 'Tube 1 – fire! Tube 2 – fire! Tube 3 – fire!'– and at the fourth ship, 'Tube 4 – fire! Rudder hard across, both engines ahead full ahead'; and up and away. *U-564* gets going flat out, and then I hear one detonation, two detonations – and at the same moment all hell breaks loose behind us. Red, green and yellow jets of flame whizz through the air. A fireball of unimaginable size lights up the night and makes the ship stand out in silhouette. Munitions have made the ship literally disintegrate; its own lethal cargo has totally destroyed it.

The pressure-wave from the explosion sweeps up behind us. A quivering orgy of colours in the sky is reflected in the water. Flying debris rains down from even more explosions, smacks into the sea all round us, and makes fountains of water shoot

Forster, Kommandant of *U-654*, is entertained aboard *U-564* soon after leaving Lorient on patrol.

up a metre high. To protect the crew from flying lumps of metal, I've sent them below. I've never seen anything like it. I am so fascinated by the sight that I stay on the bridge in the open, partially protected by the rangefinder. Brilliant flashes, sizzling, splashing, and in the background the towering column of fire. Suddenly, black as a raven, the angled bow of a frigate slides between us and the ball of fire. What's the point of having a photographer on board? This moment should be captured for posterity. I shout down, 'PK man [War Correspondent], quick, quick, to the bridge!'

No-one appears. Instead, I hear the air escaping from the dive-chambers, and notice the boat beginning to dip down at the bow. What the devil is going on? Bucketfuls of water are starting to crash onto my head as I pull the hatch shut behind me. Then the boat dives deep. I go to the Navigating Officer; I'm furious. 'Have you all taken leave of your senses? Whose job is it to give the Alarm on board? Who gave this order?' He is completely taken aback at being shouted at. 'But, Boss, you gave the order yourself – yes, the Alarm.' 'Who . . . what . . . how?' Heavens, what the poor chap has done is all perfectly reasonable. When I send the bridge watch down, as I had done in this case because of all the debris raining down, it's always the prelude to an 'Alarm' – and that is how he must have read my rather indistinct order. 'But you peasant, I didn't shout "Alarm" this time, but "PK man"' – in fact 'PK, PK.' Our stupid passenger from the Ministry of Propaganda. It was his fault that there was almost a fatal accident. So I send for him. 'I have something to say to you. You stand around and get under everyone's feet, but if there is anything out of the ordinary to film, you're nowhere to be found. You just missed a unique opportunity and it's all your own fault. What I was looking at was absolutely fantastic; it would have been the star scoop of the war, you plonker.'

The LI interrupts the dressing-down. 'Boat is at 100m'. What's next, what's going on on the surface? Have they got the escorts nearby? They're confused at the moment, which is why they haven't yet spotted us, but how long will this last? How soon will they pick up our scent, and hunt us down, like a pack of hounds after a fox? Question after question; the bottom line is – 'What are our chances of escape'? I sit in the ammunition room, between the control room and the listening room. It is so quiet in the boat that you could hear a pin drop. 'Listening room, what can you pick up?' 'Propeller noise all around; can't get a bearing on it.' Suddenly, the asdic starts – ping, ping, ping, ping. 'Flying shit, they've found us. LI, down to 150m.'

Listening room reports: 'Prop noise to port, prop noise to starboard, so many degrees'. Pinjja, pinjja, pinjja – in between, it scrapes, like a broom with iron bristles – brrt, brrt, brrt. Now the prop noises can be picked up without phones. They come from astern, pass over us and away, and fade out. Bespinn, bespinn, bespinn. All together it is an extraordinary cacophony. I suspect that it indicates a group of three corvettes. How come they don't chuck anything at us?

No sooner has the thought crossed my mind, than it happens. Five explosions, and not all that far from us. These damned depth-charges; they get more and more dangerous. In the boat everything is still OK; no leaks. But it's enough, it's quite enough. This is the work of experienced professionals; they've got their own plan worked out. 'Listening room, in a few minutes they'll attack again. To judge by the prop noise, they're coming from astern. When the escorts get close, let me know at once. LI, as soon as he makes his report, full ahead and hard a port. Pull the boat up then, and as soon as we're at 60m, blow tanks. Yes, don't look so worried; we'll chance it. We're going to surface and go for it. I'm not just going to sit here and get hammered to bits. Once we're up, diesels on and get the hell out of it! Before they've recovered from their surprise, we'll be up and away.' Behind us another five depth-charges, a bit further away. In a moment the boat comes up, as though pulled by a string. I stand under the hatch and loosen the lock. Now we're up. The fireball is still there lighting up the sky. A quick glance – I can clearly see the patrol group. They still haven't spotted us. Noisily the diesel springs into life. The distance between us and them grows – 800, 900, 1,000m. Suddenly the enemy turns in our direction. We are doing about 16 knots. 'LI, switch on the electric motors as well. Give it some acid!' Our speed rises to 17 knots; the corvettes can't keep up with us. Instead, orange flares go off overhead, and light us up. 2WO ducks automatically. Lad, lad, that won't do a lot of good! Before us a star shell lights up the low cloud. It grows as bright as if one is under a searchlight, but fades after a few seconds; the night seems even blacker than before. For a change, an explosive shell next. But we're faster, and with our low silhouette he can't target us properly. His chances are one in a thousand. The next star shell goes off just ahead of the boat, and the one after that directly over us. If that's the case, we've won the game. We're out of range of the ship, and after a few moments the darkness swallows us up. We make good our getaway.

But what's up now? Why are our diesels stopping? Monkey's up to his tricks again, I fear. Thick black smoke is coming from the exhausts. Black smoke is coming from the hatch too. A cloud of black diesel smoke is spreading out over the water, which makes it impossible to see any distance. What the devil is going on? 'Boat unfit to dive', reports the LI. What's more, the escorts are fast approaching and *U-564* can't move. 'What do you mean, "unfit to dive"? Alarm – we must dive; there is no alternative. Take her down and let's get away.' The boat manages to dive, and I can hear the electric engines starting up. But I can't believe my eyes. Standing in the central area, I can't see my hand in front of my face. There's smoke everywhere; everyone is coughing and choking. Has the lighting failed? Why hasn't the emergency lighting come on? The darkness persists, and the boat dives down. Judging by the sounds, we must be about 50–60m down. The LI is trying to get the boat level, but as he trims her *U-564* goes up at the bows again. We can't go on like that, sagging at the stern, and in the end we manage to go into a dive. The air is full of smoke, thick enough to cut with a knife. We press handkerchiefs over our noses and mouths, and some of the crew grab the emergency breathing apparatus. While we are all at sixes and sevens, the patrolling escorts are closing in at top speed, with fire in their bellies. The prop noise grows louder and louder – and then, suddenly, starts to recede! Dear God, it's incredible! Automatically everyone raises their heads and looks up – what next? No, I can't believe it! They've run over the top of us. We could hear it without the phones; they are fading away again without having a go at us. Eventually the asdic sounds – ping, ping, ping – are barely audible through the equipment and finally stop altogether. I wipe the sweat from my brow and breathe again. They've gone.

Prudence demands that we spend another quarter of an hour below the surface, despite our problems. Gradually the air clears inside the boat. The bulbs of the emergency lighting glimmer through the smoke, which is getting less now. We

Orders and reports were encoded and decoded by 'Enigma'.

turn and steer a westerly course, carefully keeping the boat level. Nothing more happens. We surface and ventilate the boat. The diesel springs into life. The smoke clears, but leaves a black film behind over everything.

'LI and mechanic to the bridge! Can you explain to me, please, exactly what the problem was? Engines out of action, and the boat full of smoke. What on earth was going on?'

'Well,' reports the LI, 'the engines stopped and a moment later everything was dark in the boat. I was about to go into the engine-room to investigate when you gave the alarm, so I stayed in the control room at my dive station.' It is the mechanic who finally sheds light on the whole thing. It was what is often called Sod's Law, a combination of circumstances. Someone had left a handful of oily rags lying on a ledge directly over the bend in the exhaust pipe. While we were being chased, what with the twisting and turning of the boat the rags fell off, down onto the exhaust pipe, which was glowing red-hot with the speed we were moving at; so the rags caught fire and fell into the bilge. By that stage of the patrol a fair bit of oil was swilling around in there, which turned it immediately into a full-scale blaze. They opened the outside ventilation valve and flooded the bilge. The fire was quickly out, and we surfaced soon afterwards. Small cause, but with dramatic effects. This time we got away with it; but the boat is a real mess. The U-boat looks like a blackened oil-lamp. It isn't however as dangerous as it looks, in the opinion of the LI, who is waiting for me in the wardroom. Good; I give orders for him to issue cleaning materials to the whole crew, and they can each get rid of the mess around their own station. Is my corner clean enough yet for me to sit down in?

Afterwards, I give the cook orders to prepare a special celebration 'coffee-party', regardless of the state of the crew's rations, which are being carefully conserved. I let the mechanic, Kräh, sit next to me, and I make a proper little 'speech from the scaffold'. 'Listen in, you two. It's perfectly clear to me that God didn't just have a hand in this but an entire arm. Fire on board and diesels U/S, so that we were immobilised; had the escort group realised what had happened to us, our last hour would have come. If we didn't have a crew so well-trained that it could do everything in the dark, there's no telling what might have happened. Nobody got too stressed or even out-of-breath, and the LI handled the boat in an irreproachable manner. It was a remarkable achievement. No; I

Suhren cuts the celebration cake after the engine-room fire.

can celebrate our success with the rest of the crew – even the mutton-head who left his cleaning rags on the ledge by the exhaust. I don't wish to know who he is; I hope he has learned his lesson. Pass me the mike. Captain to crew: Everyone of you has done his best and helped to sort the boat out – including the one who was responsible for setting fire to it. It could have been a real crisis, but as far as I'm concerned I'm really proud of my crew. And now I'm going to have a lie-down.'

The diesels chug away. The watch goes up to the bridge. We cruise as usual on a three-watch system. The Navigating Officer puts us on course for the refuelling position. *U-564* is going to meet the 'Milch Cow'. My legs are worn out with standing all day, and back-pain keeps me awake as well now. Also my nerves are jangling with the strong coffee. So I doze a bit, and think back over the last few hours again. Under the circumstances my decision to surface and make a getaway was the right one. Of course it could have been a disaster. But if one's going to cop it, then better be on the surface than below it.

Erich Topp, colleague and friend of Suhren throughout the war.

Bridge announces, 'Dawn approaching'. While I am trying to get dressed – and feel all my aches – a new report comes in. 'Mastheads to Port'. I'm still in pyjamas, so I throw a jacket over the top and go up on the bridge. Yes, in fact two funnels. What is the course of the freighter? The WO isn't too sure, he doesn't answer. We pass the funnels and turn. The funnels don't move from the spot. Unless it's a big liner . . . But it isn't; as it dawns the 'ghost' turns into two Azores fishermen. Their sails gradually emerge from the grey of the night. What now, back on the old course? A vague unease holds me back. 'Control room, pass my 8x60 binoculars up to the bridge'.

It takes a minute to focus; then what I see in the eyepiece makes me stop breathing, and shout 'Alarm!' Behind the Azores fishing boats I can clearly see the stepped outlines of two warships. Once down below the surface, I keep them in the periscope for a while. Distance 10–12 nautical miles. They're enormous ships. In daylight they grow bigger still – super-huge, to coin a phrase. They are battleships. If they carry on in my direction, I'll be in a good position to take a shot at them. But they don't do me any favours; they make a sharp tack and turn away to the west. Both engines full ahead; let's see if we can get a bit nearer. After a minute, slow ahead and periscope up. The battleships are still travelling westwards and four destroyers are providing an escort for them. Together they make a regular battle formation. Are they aware of us? Quite possibly – the group turns north and cruises off at 18 knots. About 2,000m outside the range of our torpedoes they pass by us without stopping. Both my WOs have a look at them in the periscope. A double like this would have done us nicely! There's no possibility of it, though; we can't go fast enough under water. As the group vanishes over the horizon, we surface and send in a report of our sighting of the enemy, and of their intended course and speed. About the class of ship we can't be sure. The BdU asks us whether they could have been the *Nelson* and the *Rodney*, two of the most powerful British warships afloat. As it was to turn out later, that's exactly what they were. It had been a sight for the Gods. Never again I would see the like of it at sea. The firework display of the blazing munitions ship was a unique experience. Pictures of that night etched themselves indelibly on my mind. The shadows of the escorts, the star shells above us; but all this would soon be a thing of the past as far as I was concerned. The sequences kept rolling, like something out of a war film, but they were beginning to come to an end. This journey to the Caribbean was to be my last patrol, and then I wouldn't have to go on taking any more risks.

At our last meeting the BdU said to me, 'Suhren, make sure you bring your boat safely back, and then come ashore. Then we can use you back at home for training. Prien, Kretschmer and Schepke would in theory have been ideal for the job, but they are all gone. Prien and Schepke are dead, Kretschmer has been taken prisoner. Topp has already come ashore – and you're next.' I venture an objection:' Admiral, in my opinion an assignment like that isn't the right thing for me.' He cuts me short; 'Suhren, every month new boats are commissioned. We need an experienced man to train the crews.' And with that I was more or less excused there and then from front-line duty. Just one more voyage, this one, my fifteenth patrol. My crew had no idea of this, and I intended to conceal it from them as long as possible, so as not to cause any premature loss of morale. They would miss me, and would begin to worry about who might be taking over. Their lives frequently depended on their having an experienced commander.

9

In Colombus' waters – Between tropical magic and the wet abyss – The captain's swords – A nasty accident

'STÜRKORL' DOES A FIRST-CLASS job with the navigation. Without having to search around for long, we meet up with the supply boat in the pre-arranged quadrant: a tiny point in the endless ocean. The 'Milch Cow' – *U-459*. She is driven by one of the oldest captains, who was actually in the First World War, KK Georg Graf von Wilamowitz-Möllendorf, better known to us as 'Wild Moritz'. We greet each other with semaphore flags, 'C to C' etc. It's like waiting for the pump at a petrol station. Everyone wants to be first. Still, our rendezvous is well away from other ships in the middle of the peaceful 'gap', out of reach of any plane. The aircraft carriers of the enemy (and there still aren't many of them) are otherwise engaged. Unless a destroyer stumbles on us, we can lie here undetected. However, a long-distance traveller is always in a hurry. It's been arranged for another boat to link up before us, and we are supposed to take our turn; but the other boat doesn't trust itself to pick up the lines, because there is a bit of a sea running. Why couldn't we have been first? We paddle in our inflatable dinghy, in sea-state 4/5, backwards and forwards from submarine to submarine bobbing about like a cork on the waves. The inflatable came from an airman who had been shot down in the North Sea. Taken on board as a souvenir, as it were, it had become the captain's gig.

And we were going to have to wait here for a good while yet. My patience was running out, so I said to Wilamowitz, 'Could

The navigating officer of *U-564* ('Stürkorl') at his desk.

you ask the other boat whether we can get on with it before him?' Wilamowitz signalled back; 'Lend me your heavy gun; I'll soon get rid of him!' In the end the other one gives up and clears out of the area. Carefully I connect *U-564* to the 'Milch Cow', with a line to her stern, and in no time we have the hose across. We transfer the stores in the inflatable. We get going with the business of transferring 50 tons of diesel, along with enough fresh water and provisions for the Caribbean – for Columbus

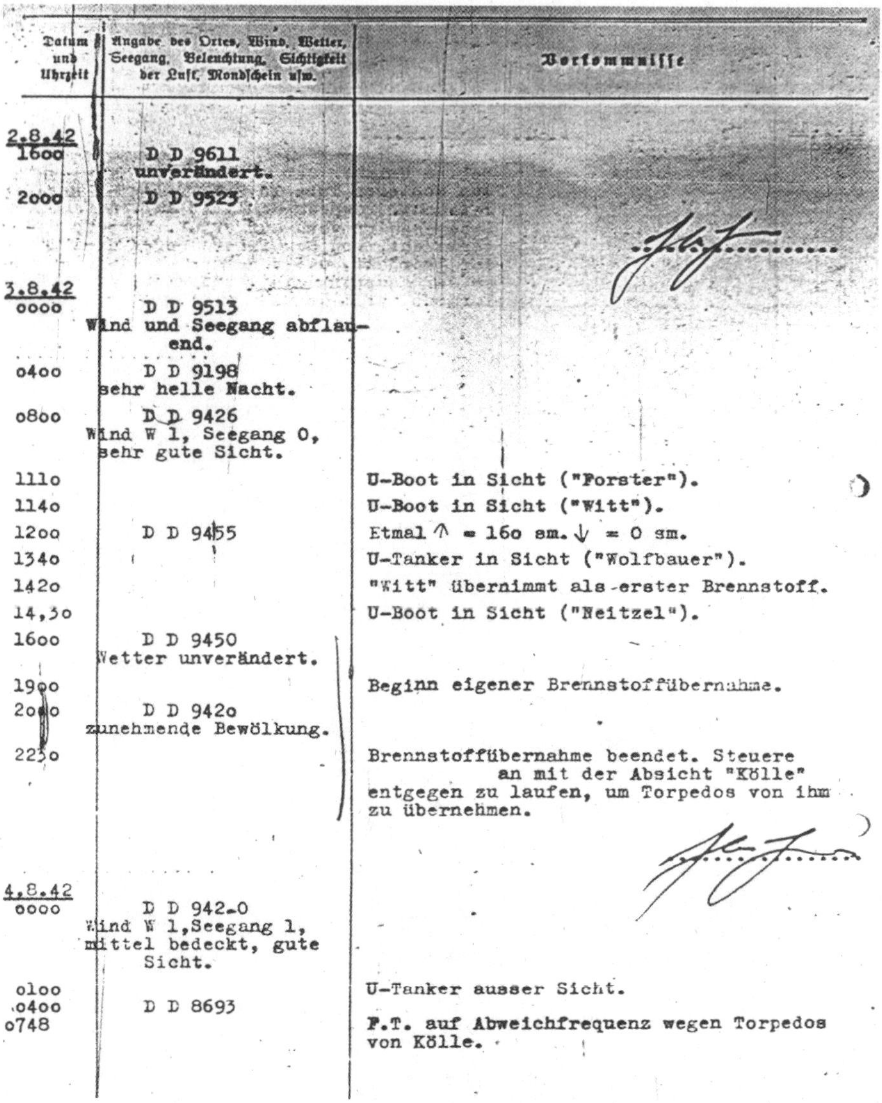

Datum und Uhrzeit	Angabe des Ortes, Wind, Wetter, Seegang, Beleuchtung, Sichtigkeit der Luft, Mondschein usw.	Vorkommnisse
2.8.42 1600	D D 9611 unverändert.	
2000	D D 9523	
3.8.42 0000	D D 9513 Wind und Seegang abflauend.	
0400	D D 9198 sehr helle Nacht.	
0800	D D 9426 Wind W 1, Seegang 0, sehr gute Sicht.	
1110		U-Boot in Sicht ("Forster").
1140		U-Boot in Sicht ("Witt").
1200	D D 9455	Etmal ↑ = 160 sm. ↓ = 0 sm.
1340		U-Tanker in Sicht ("Wolfbauer").
1420		"Witt" übernimmt als erster Brennstoff.
14,30		U-Boot in Sicht ("Neitzel").
1600	D D 9450 Wetter unverändert.	
1900		Beginn eigener Brennstoffübernahme.
2000	D D 9420 zunehmende Bewölkung.	
2230		Brennstoffübernahme beendet. Steuere an mit der Absicht "Kölle" entgegen zu laufen, um Torpedos von ihm zu übernehmen.
4.8.42 0000	D D 942.0 Wind W 1, Seegang 1, mittel bedeckt, gute Sicht.	
0100		U-Tanker ausser Sicht.
0400	D D 8693	
0748		F.T. auf Abweichfrequenz wegen Torpedos von Kölle.

A page from the log of *U-564*, recording the rendezvous with the 'Milch Cow' and the transfer of torpedoes in August 1942. Letters and numbers (*eg* DD 9611) give their position on the grid map of the Atlantic used by all U-boats. Suhren's signature appears at the end of each day's report, which was typed up on board by the radio operator. The log was handed in at the end of the patrol for inspection, and ultimately a written comment by Dönitz himself.

territory! So far so good. The only thing we're missing, on this last patrol of mine, is the batch of four torpedoes which we've used in the unscheduled attack on the convoy. Where can we get some, short of stealing them? In a reply from the BdU, I learn that there is a boat heading home which might be able to let us have some torpedoes. The only problem, however, is that we have no crane to transfer them with. We would have to improvise something. This results in an excited discussion with the crew, the outcome of which is that we devise a clever method of transferring torpedoes from one boat to another at sea without the use of a mechanism or any special apparatus. Later on, after it was all over, I was often asked, 'How on earth did you do it without any assistance? How come the torpedoes didn't sink?' For a torpedo doesn't normally float; it's more in the nature of a dynamically propelled projectile; as soon as it stops it will sink. Its weight in water is around 100–120 kilos, a fact that it is important to know.

We met the captain of the homeward-bound boat at a prearranged time and place, and the first thing he did was ask me the same question. By a quirk of fate he turned out to have previously been my divisional officer at the Naval Academy at Mürwik, where they had taken such pains to prepare me for the officers' exam. He was the one who had given me the hardest time despite my being one of the best. On that day, though, he gazed stupidly at me as I stood there with decorations up to my chin. It was quite a reunion! When I asked him why he was intending to go home with all his torpedoes still on board, he replied that it was because he was ill: he had a liver problem and needed to get to a doctor. 'Oh, I see, belly-ache; spare me the details. Now, let's get the things over here.'

So I and some of my crew swam across to his boat and tied lifejackets all along the torpedo. Yes, lifejackets! One jacket can support 10 kilos, and with more lifejackets we provided enough support for a torpedo to stay afloat under our watchful eyes. Then, with *U-564* alongside, we pulled the torpedoes across with blocks and lines one after the other. On our foredeck was fitted a cradle, which we had used in harbour for letting the torpedoes slide into the boat. So the order was given, 'LI, let the bows dip, so that the foredeck is under water'. After we'd pulled the floating torpedo across and over the cradle with the lines, the order was given to surface, so that the cradle came up to grip the torpedo. The next bit all had to be done very fast. 'Torpedo hatch open', and the eel slipped down the sloping cradle on its own into the boat. Tackle away, torpedo hatch closed again. Next please. Pulling lines and blocks. Dip the bows, get it over the cradle, up again; one by one we get the eels in. I stand by with a boathook to help if there's a hitch.

All went brilliantly right up to the last one. We'd forgotten one small detail: namely that lifejackets always lose a bit of air, and hence lift. We should have kept blowing them up again in between times. Suddenly the fourth torpedo stood on its head, and we had to literally let it drop. Away it went, down to 5,000m. Well, they say there's no such thing as the perfect crime. As I've said, a good deal was said about the exploit afterwards. But one thing we never let on: that we'd already spent a day practising the whole thing down to the last detail, moving one of our torpedoes from the stern to the bows and back again. In the event, the whole thing went like clockwork!

We had passed the island of Tobago, and sailed west into the Caribbean, a setting for pirates, sunken treasure galleons and Spanish colonialism, of tropical magic and island romance. But most of this was history, and the only romance was now well and truly in the past. War – and after all, this was what we were living through – is always grim and bloody. An unbearable heat came off the boat during the day, though the breeze from astern brought a bit of cool relief. One day I sat with the LI in the wardroom making plans, and sniffed. 'Tell me, Gabler, can you smell anything? Isn't that freighter smoke? Let's see go up on deck and see what's happening.' Over us, the blue-black night, silver moonlight on the sea, and good visibility. I couldn't believe my eyes. On the starboard quarter, about 5,000–6,000m off, and clearly visible without the glasses, was the shadow of a big freighter. The night was definitely too bright for a surface attack; we would have been spotted as we approached.

'Action stations, both engines half-ahead.' Cautiously we follow the zigzag course of the other ship, which allows us to overtake it comfortably and finally watch it from ahead. We dive carefully. I hang onto the periscope, and report the course and the timings of the turns so as to work out our shot. The freighter stands there big and black before my eyes. The listening-room takes a bearing on it too. 'Now, Nav. Officer, how's that, shouldn't we turn towards it?' 'No, Boss, not yet'. But a few minutes later, 'Now!' We swing onto the target. 'Prepare torpedo for firing, enemy ship bearing 060 degrees, speed 12 knots. Ready to fire, tube 3: stand by, tube 3 – fire!' 'Stürkorl' stares at the stopwatch and counts. Soon, it all happens. The bow of the freighter moves across my field of view, and crosses into the torpedoes path. A few heartbeats more, and then a boom – detonation! Exactly amidships. The cargo burns

Torpedoes are transferred to *U-564* (note the lifejackets).

The 'Gap' – the mid-Atlantic was not yet covered by planes.

brightly. We surface and through the smoke we land a few 8.8cm shells on him. Behind her two more ships must have thought they were for it.

U-564 is cruising in one of the most beautiful areas of the Caribbean, in a little corner of the Little Antilles, between the Windward Islands and Leeward Islands. The North East trade-wind blows reliably all year and is at its strongest in the evening, when it takes away the heat of the day before drop-

A U-boat under heavy aerial attack.

ping at night. The names of the islands could have been taken from exotic novels or a tourist brochure. They fire the imagination: Antigua, Guadeloupe, Dominica, Martinique, St Lucia. We cross from Margarita, the island of pearls, to Cuba, the assembly point of the Spanish silver fleet. We make a detour to Curacao, where oil is shipped from Venezuela, and from where we suspect the big tankers come. But though there is a lot of bright light, there is also a lot of shadow, and the serene summer picture is marred by oil, blood and the wrecks of steel ships. Well, I didn't start the war. There's not a lot of point in worrying about it. If you do that, you've had it – you won't be much longer for this life. My philosophising in this evening hour is quickly terminated by the warning cry 'Plane!'.

I leave my corner in the control room to go to the bridge, but two sharp detonations shake the boat hard. Through the round opening of the hatch, I see from below as though

Gabler congratulates Suhren on his promotion.

Suhren gives his crew a pep-talk before the final run for home.

through a large telescope the wing of a plane passing overhead. It's just missed us. 'Alarm!' I turn the valves on the forward dive cells myself, having got there before the man whose job it is to attend to them. The bow dips down, and in record time – under half a minute – we are below the surface. 'Dive, dive, dive.' *U-564* shoots headfirst into the depths at a sharp angle driven by the electric motors. 30, 40 – but at 50m a detonation hits us with the power of a steam hammer and just about lifts us off our feet. Question: 'Leaks?' Bow and stern report 'All OK'. LI reports, 'Boat is at 60m, flooding trim cells and levelling her off'. If that's the case, what's going on? Do my ears deceive me? Along with the usual noise of the boat I am picking up that typical crackling noise that starts when the boat overshoots the 120m mark and begins to crack up under the huge pressure of water on the framework. Something's wrong; the depth-gauge is giving a false reading. The boat is plunging down into the bottomless depths, into the watery abyss. I shout out – 'Both rudders hard up, blow for'ard.' We must try to get the bows up with compressed air. The ventilation valve is still open; in his panic the man is turning it the wrong way, until I push him out of the light. The crackling of the frames grows even louder, as the ship's mate lets compressed air into the dive-chamber. Our hair stands on end. According to the meter on the trim-chamber, we're already at 160m, and the boat is still down at the bow. There's no stopping it. I wonder frantically whether I could stop it by going full astern. It would be pointless; it wouldn't achieve anything. But at last, by the time we reach 180m the boat is gradually beginning to lift its head up. We are already at the danger point, but we still go on sinking to 200m. And always that horrible creaking and crackling as though a giant's fist was trying to crush the boat. Finally, we manage to level it out with the depth-rudder. The situation gets back to normal. The LI checks over the depth gauge, and it seems as though with the hard knocks the boat has taken, the pointer has come adrift from the drive shaft and hasn't been turning with it any more. Consequence, nearly

Pennants hoisted on the boat's return marked Allied ships claimed as sunk (here by *U-564*).

total destruction in the depths. The gauge had given up. The men in the engine-room explain that before diving they had seen a jet of flame come through the torpedo hatch, and that the hatch must be damaged. I am pretty sceptical, but I suppose it could be right. The second serious attack came when we were already at 50m, when the instruments fixed to the bulkhead were torn off; and we did find later that the torpedo tube was flooded. The watch on the bridge apologised for the fact that the aircraft had come at them straight out of the evening sun, which was why they had spotted it too late. But one can hardly blame them for that.

I decide to remain submerged during the day. Otherwise the watch on the bridge have to remain alert to everything and the demands on them are too great. It is too much for the men. The grilling sun, the brightness on the sea, the blistering heat, all combine to make the concentration seize up. Conditions in the Caribbean are quite different to those in the Atlantic. I shall avoid taking any risks, and dive by day. In the safety of the deep I can rely on the listening-room, which can let me know of any propeller noise, and the crew can relax. And even if the sweat does trickle from every pore, at least the water isn't too cold!

At night we surface, and my place is on the bridge. I am in the middle of a watch one night, when the same thing happens again. Another boat reports a contact: convoy in quadrant so-and-so, speed 10 knots, course northeast. According to the Nav. Officer the convoy should be in sight round about 05.00 local time, so I go below and have a lie down. The radio operator is supposed to wake me at the right time. Later, around 03.00, I wake up, turn over and try to go back to sleep. But I begin to wonder why I am so wide awake if nothing is up? On the bridge a cool wind blows in my face and freshens me up as we cruise. 'Have you seen anything?' 'No, not a thing.' There's still a bit of time to go. I take a look through the glasses, as a matter of routine since nothing is happening. A glance behind us and I am thunderstruck. That has to be . . . 'Look, you lot,

U-564 re-enters a U-boat pen at Brest after her patrol.

the entire convoy is steaming along behind us; it's just about on top of us! What the devil's happened to your eyes?' The WO and the look-outs gaze in the direction I mean, but they can't make anything out. I give orders to turn in that direction, and after a while the silhouettes appear over the horizon; I can clearly see the escorts. Either my crew have gone blind, or they are not used to the tropics! But now isn't the time to discuss it. The sky's just beginning to turn grey, and with the short dawn in the tropics it will soon be light. So I give orders to dive, and settle down again.

The convoy steams on as though pulled on a string. It's daylight now. The torpedoes are ready, the four tubes are trained on the freighters. Range 1,200m. We send off the first. We clearly hear a loud bang – but no detonation. The other eels don't work either. One of the freighters stops and I see through the periscope the crew bending over the rails amidships. There doesn't seem to be any damage, otherwise the ship wouldn't still be hanging about as a target. They must be looking at the place where the torpedo has hit them: but it's not gone off. The four torpedoes that we went to all that trouble to get on board in the Atlantic are duds. The complicated mechanics of a torpedo – control system, rudder mechanism and detonator – simply couldn't stand jolts as hard as those inflicted by the bombs dropped from the aeroplane. (That's my own opinion, anyway, which was confirmed later in the Straits of Florida when three warships slipped through my fingers.) The planes were equipped with depth-charges specially designed to be air-dropped, vastly superior to their earlier ones. We only succeed now in sinking two freighters travelling alone, and then we head off home. It was been my last and longest journey.

We had by now spent over two months at sea, had carried out our mission, and could afford to look after ourselves a bit. In the 'gap' in the air-cover, *U-564* took a break, to give the crew the opportunity to bathe in the deep-blue Atlantic again. But not to court disaster – like Mützelburg – by diving in head-first. In the meantime, one of the WOs and an off-watch mate

A hero's welcome awaited Suhren and the crew.

had orders to arm themselves with machine guns and be on the look-out for sharks. I didn't want to make a present of my crew to the fishes for lunch through not taking precautions. Our mere presence there was dangerous enough. After this break for recuperation we set off for home.

One day I had just sat down in the wardroom and was going over the events of the day in my mind, when the diesels suddenly stopped. There was an extraordinary quiet all over the boat. As quick as a flash I remember the fire on board, and though we were at that point out of the range of British fighter-planes, being motionless was quite worrying enough. But as I hastily entered the control room, my anxieties vanished. My LI announced, beaming with delight, that all the crew had gone up on deck to congratulate me. 'To congratulate me? Why?' I bounded up onto the bridge. There stood most of the crew, grinning from ear to ear, and the LI was holding several decoded signals in his hand. He did his best to read them out with sufficient dignity: –

'In recognition of your proven heroism, you are the 18th member of the German Armed Forces to whom I grant Crossed Swords to your Knight's Cross with Oak Leaves. Adolf Hitler'.

And the next – 'I am delighted to be able to inform you, with my heartfelt good wishes, of your promotion to Korvettenkapitän, in token of your exceptionally distinguished service against the enemy. Oberbefehlshaber Raeder.'

Congratulations followed from the BdU, from my Flotilla and from Konteradmiral Saalwächter. They'd managed to keep all the signals back and collect them together to surprise me. What's more, the workshop had made new rings for me to wear from tin cans, and even a set of broad Oak Leaves for my officer's cap. In front of all the crew my LI decorated me with them, and with that the little improvised ceremony came to an end. The diesels came back to life.

There I sat, on 1 September 1942, at twenty-six a KK as well as decorated with the highest possible award for bravery. Under any other circumstances I would have been perfectly happy with just one of the two! As things were, I took hold of the mike to announce over the tannoy; 'A boat is only as good as its crew, but its crew is only as good as its captain. You know that I have never undertaken – or ordered you to undertake – any lunatic exploits that might result in you risking your necks. Nevertheless, with your help I have been able to explore the limits of what is possible. For that I thank you all. In fourteen days at the most we shall be home, and we shall see to that now as our next priority.' I thought of Dönitz's words: 'Suhren, make sure you bring your boat back again in one piece.'

The visibility was so good that one could see any circling aircraft in good time and dive out of sight. The last test awaiting us was the Bay of Biscay. Although we had got through it previously at full speed and on the surface, I wasn't much in favour of this tactic now. The accuracy with which the planes had flown at us made me assume that the enemy had radar now fitted to their planes in spite of all expectations to the contrary,

Flowers marked the Kommandant's safe return.

and that they could pin-point us on the surface. Not in all aircraft, perhaps, but certainly in those squadrons which were involved in submarine pursuit. It would only take a plane like that to appear suddenly through the cloud above us, and not even prayer and evasive tactics would do any good. We'd be bombed before we knew anything about it.

So, under a moderately high alto-stratus we dived for safety and collected in the listening room. We were just off the tip of the mainland of Europe, where the deep Atlantic rises in steps to 200m. By night we surfaced cautiously and took a look. There were now seven men on the bridge. Apart from me there were the two WOs, Lawetz and Waldschmitt, the bosuns Webendorfer, Bartels, Thiel and Able Seaman Schmutzler. All were good and experienced look-outs. However, with a crowd of seven up top, an emergency dive would now inevitably be almost impossible. Nevertheless, I was happy with things as they were, and kept the boat on the surface. We ploughed on through the Bay of Biscay at 15 knots, at least double the speed we would have made had we been submerged. Two hours later Schmutzler spotted a huge flying-boat coming from the starboard side, not far off and only about 150m above the sea. 'Get below, get below!' The plane hung about, but spotted nothing. We stayed at 50m for the rest of the night: best to be safe. On the last day at sea we had excellent visibility. The planes didn't stop bothering us, though, and towards dusk drove us down half-a-dozen times.

In quiet moments 'Stürkorl' could again take a midday fix, and once it was dark enough he could take the elevations of two fixed stars and determine our position exactly. Before we spent our last night down below we gave notice of our ETA and the position at which we expected to encounter the escort which was coming out to meet us. When we surface at dawn we can see the blockade-breaker and two minesweepers which are there to protect us and bring us into harbour. All of the crew who do not have duties below are ordered to fall in on deck and to enjoy the fresh air, and to stay on deck as far as possible, just in case at the last minute . . .

In front the high coast of Brittany appears. Out of the mist looms the town of Brest, with its broad roads and narrow harbour entrance. The landmarks appear, the harbour basin, the Arsenal, on the left the Naval College and the U-boat bunkers. A launch filled with officer friends from the 1st

Flotilla came out to meet us, and with them the Flotilla Surgeon, Dr Richter. He was pretty impressed. In spite of my absence of three months my men looked healthy and cheerful: their hair was cut, beards trimmed, green on-board uniform painstakingly cleaned.

I felt in some way as though I was a different person. The officers standing around me seemed more distant, their laughter more remote. But it was really no different from normal. After previous shorter patrols I hadn't felt the same way, this sensation of 'being apart'. Perhaps the stress of all those weeks of being responsible for them hadn't worn off yet. But the feeling of being isolated didn't go away. A swig from an offered bottle of brandy didn't help much either. The long period of temperance had dramatic consequences. The stuff tasted horrible and took effect immediately. The adjutant delays the boat's arrival; we have to wait until the reception ceremony is sorted out. Eventually a message in morse is received, '*U-564*, you can come in now'.

Just before reaching the pierhead we switched from noisy diesels to e-motors, and slid easily into the harbour basin. On the pier was drawn up the Army Band, a Naval Guard of Honour, the Town Mayor with his wife, a crowd of army officers, soldiers in grey and blue, and port-employees who had knocked off for a moment. Hands waving, flowers. Brest is a tidal harbour, the water level goes up and down, so in front of the jetty was moored a barge to serve as a pontoon to tie up to. On that the chief of the flotilla was waiting for us. Near him stood my friend Hein Uphoff (*U-84*) who had got there just ahead of me. In the mess he was in the habit of telling rude but really very funny jokes about the Nazis. His face looked drawn as though he'd had a hard night. It made me ask him, with the megaphone pointed at him, 'Well, Hein, are the Nazis still at the helm then?' The flotilla chief jerked to attention and saluted: but he had heard the remark more clearly than he should have. Eventually, the story spread right round the fleet without doing me any harm. Even nowadays I get reminded of it!

Zweibrücken, 2.1.1942

The crew of *U-564* on leave during the war at their affiliated town of Zweibrücken.

Both engines half astern. The way came off the boat and *U-564* came alongside with a slight bump. The music started up, and the flotilla-chief came over the gangway and came on board with measured step. Attention! We pay our respects to him. 'Report *U-564* returning from patrol'. Handshakes; congratulations. In deference to my new status the flotilla had produced ceremonial swords specially made of tropical wood, which they presented with suitable words. 'Fitting for the whole flotilla to pay tribute, etc etc'. The hatchway in the barge was covered over with planks, and the whole thing was covered over with an awning to keep the rain off. The crowd on the pier pressed closer, and a group of army officers suddenly hurried in their enthusiasm on to what was supposed to be a roof. Under their weight the whole thing began to break up and fall apart. The music got more and more anguished and finally all of a sudden ground to a halt. The Commander shouted 'Call the ambulances!' Everything was happening at once. No one had reckoned with an accident like this. The Flotilla Chief had tried at the last moment to raise his arms to gesture to the soldiers to stay back, because he could see disaster looming.

But in vain! My crew and the flotilla personnel helped clear away the debris. The doctor and his staff attended to the worst injured as best they could in the emergency, putting on bandages and stopping the bleeding. Ambulances arrived tooting their horns. The pier was closed off. The infantry regiment had just arrived here from Russia to recuperate. But what a terrible reception; even in port *U-564* did pretty well for excitement!

10

Ashore after my fifteenth patrol – From Reichkanzlei to Obersalzberg – 'Submarine Swing' with Eva Braun – Bormann: 'Suhren, I like you more by the minute'

AS USUAL I WENT TO meet the BdU, Dönitz, in Paris for a debrief. Among other things we talked in due course about the fire on the boat, and I couldn't help including the comment of my Nav. Officer, which had reduced the tension in the atmosphere considerably at the time. The enemy corvettes had just left us, the danger was receding, but we were still groping around in the dark and were feeling very much under pressure. The Navigating Officer had given vent to his feelings by calling out loud and clear, so as to be clearly audible through the entire boat, 'It's as dark in here as a bear's arse'. Unfortunately this rich remark didn't quite produce the same humorous effect in Paris that it had on board. Dönitz, who still towered over me sitting down, looked me up and down wryly for a while and commented, 'Was it really as dark as that in there?' I knew that he wasn't keen on that sort of language; I'd already provoked his displeasure as a young lieutenant during our first meeting on board *U-48* by swearing during gunnery practice and answering him back when reproved.

At the end of the debriefing, which covered the highlights of the problems we encountered during the attack on the convoy, Dönitz went on, 'Suhren, you are the most experienced of all my captains. Now, give me an answer to this question: does the enemy have radar? Think carefully before you reply.'

This had been the most important question recently under discussion: whether radar was being installed in planes – which was held by our side to be a technological impossibility. But now, I didn't need to think for long; the facts spoke for themselves. For example, the attack of the four-engine Liberator, which, after I had turned away through 90 degrees, went on following my old course with its searchlight and promptly lost me. It must have picked me up on its radar and had only failed to notice just for a moment when I changed course. Later in the Bay of Biscay, in pitch-darkness, I was again targeted by a Sunderland coming straight at me; I was only able to evade it in the nick of time through the alertness of my lookouts. So I replied, 'Sir, as far as I'm concerned, it's clear that they do carry radar in their planes. I don't know how they've managed to do it, but they've got it. Perhaps not in every plane yet, but soon they'll all be equipped with it, and then our submarines are going to have a hard time dealing with the problem of air-surveillance'.

And that turned out to be the case. They principally used a centimetre-wave position-finder to track us down. Our later radar-detectors, called Metox or Naxos, which only a few boats carried, were in my experience the only useful form of protection. The same applied even more to the initially improvised 'Biscay Cross', a primitive and cumbersome wooden framework that produced a continuous 'peeping' sound, and had to be dismantled for an emergency-dive. Its cable however had to be led down through the open hatch, and an obstructed hatch can be fatal.

Dönitz was very concerned, and relayed this back to his Chief of Staff, Kapitän zur See Godt and his Radio Consultant, KK Meckel. But nothing altered regarding my assignment. On the contrary – 'You with your rude health have managed to survive fifteen patrols. In the future we shall be building new boats, and I need you with your experience to train up the new crews. Erich Topp has also come ashore and won't be doing any more patrols either'. And I got one more warning as we left: 'Suhren, you are now a prominent figure, with all your decorations, whom people will listen to. Think carefully before you open your mouth, and choose your language more carefully.'

As I have already mentioned, after our meeting with Dönitz we usually made our way to the Scheherezade. I was always welcomed there with open arms. The band started up by playing my favourite song – 'Je t'aime'. But as far as I was concerned no other voice was good enough; my girlfriend Monique was not there. Tamara and Pati were as cheerful as ever but laid down clear limits. So in view of our unavoidable separation Paris for me finished up in a minor key.

My departure from 'my' boat, and I mean from 'my' boat, was not too painful. I hadn't become too attached to it, as was the case with many. My relationship with it was purely professional. The most important thing to me was the personnel on board. The boat itself was no more than a means to an end, but the fact that I was able to make such good use of it was due entirely to the skill of these individuals. The majority of the young men were barely over twenty, and I was not a lot older myself. After we had had the fire on board, the Leading Mechanic had recommended putting the culprit on report and punishing him formally because of the danger to which he had exposed the crew. But I refused to put him on report. 'Report?', I said; 'that is the last thing I'd think of doing. First, he wouldn't be the only one, and it wasn't intentional; and second, he would have gone down with the others himself. So let's leave it alone and forget about it; what's done is done.'

But leaving my crew lay heavy on my heart. When my LI Oberleutnant Gabler spoke to the crew assembled in front of the dais at the Naval Academy, I got such a lump in my throat that I couldn't manage to get a word out. I turned eventually to Gabler and asked him to send them to my room one at a time so that I could shake each of them by the hand for the last time. So I did see them all once again. All went well, until it came to the orphan, Able Seaman Schmutzler, to whom, young as I was, I had become a kind of parent. He began to sob, and kept repeating through his tears, 'I have no-one any more, I have no-one any more.' I was deeply moved myself. I tried to comfort him; 'Listen, if ever you're in a spot of bother and need help, you can always come to me and I'll see what I can do. But as for taking you with me – no, that's out of the question.' I could breathe freely again once it was all over. I scarcely saw anyone from my old crew again. Over a long period I ran into one or two, like 'Stürkorl' Limburg, whom I met in Hamburg, and helmsman Grünert. Most of them fell in the war – as did Able Seaman Schmutzler.

The boat belonged to the 1st Flotilla. I handed it over without great ceremony into the care of 1WO Lawetz and 2WO Waldschmitt. The new captain of *U-564* was Oberleutnant Fiedler. He didn't achieve any more successes with her, and she was badly damaged on 14 June 1943 by a British bomber and sank under their feet. Fiedler went to *U-333*, formerly the boat of Ali Cremer, and three weeks later was lost on his first patrol with her. The good old days had come to an end; the chances of surviving, as I've said before, had become very slim.

My LI Gabler came ashore at the same time as I did. He was due to come ashore one patrol earlier, but I'd objected strongly to that, and warned von Friedeburg, 'If you take Gabler away from me, I shall refuse to go to sea any more myself. We are used to working together; in fact we have a perfect working relationship. He often acts on his own initiative without my needing to give him orders. I could never adapt to working with a young and inexperienced LI.' And because in the meantime I had become a 'distinguished figure, to whom people listened', I managed to get my own way. Now we were both ashore. As a former boat-builder, Gabler moved to a technical unit in the Hartz where new types of U-boat were designed. Eventually that was where the wooden 1:1 model of a hydrogen-driven Walther submarine of Type XXVI, the newest of the new, fell into the hands of the Russians – the

Americans had to leave it behind, because they didn't know what to do with it. (The Russians of course didn't either!)

Gabler also was one of the few with whom I met up again long after the war. He was a real expert, having already designed submarines abroad between the wars. He set up his own agency for engineers, employing many other assistants, and was heavily involved with the construction of all the new types of submarine in Western Europe.

When I returned to Berlin in the sleeping car, I left an eventful period of my life behind me; but as the wheels continued to turn I didn't have long to think about the past. I arrived at the capital city of the Reich fresh and rested; the supreme commander of the Navy, Großadmiral Raeder, had invited me to have breakfast with various others in the Kaiserhof. I wasn't too keen on the Kaiserhof. I'd had a bit of trouble there early on. On the occasion of the award of the Oak Leaves, I had

The Kaiserhof in Berlin.

Suhren (r) and Topp (centre) inspecting an anti-aircraft gun.

stayed there with Lehmann-Willenbrock and spent the night in the famous Jockey Bar. The Jockey Bar closed at 4am and continued until 8 for hotel guests only. When we finally got back to the Kaiserhof, we felt a terrible thirst coming on, and ordered some soda water. But they wouldn't serve us. They told us that this was no time for soda-water or any nonsense of that sort. There was nothing we could do about it; they simply ignored us. It was like talking to a brick wall. 'Fine', I said in the end, 'that's it for the Kaiserhof as far as I'm concerned. I'm not a Party member, so as a simple naval officer I seem to be doomed to play second fiddle here. As you wish, gentlemen; I'll be off, and find lodgings elsewhere.'

As is common knowledge, the Kaiserhof was 'brown' through and through. That was where they all sat in state. Hitler had stayed there with his closest staff before he came to power – about which Goebbels wrote a book, much read at the time, called *From Kaiserhof to Chancellor of the Reich.* We on the other hand were a quite different colour, wore blue uniform, and were suspected of being 'too blue'. After that I changed from the Kaiserhof to the Hotel Adlon. There, 'Unter den Linden', I was well looked after. The first time I stayed at the Adlon, a pageboy appeared. 'Herr Adlon presents his compliments and wonders when it would be convenient to pay his respects to you.' Now that was certainly flattering, but 'due courtesy where courtesy is due'; we had been brought up to do things a certain way, and as far as I was concerned it was the younger who should pay his respects to the older. So I asked permission to visit him. From then on a personal friendship developed between me and the aristocratic and white-haired Herr Adlon, who knew how to conduct himself properly with Kings and Princes. This continued until things fell apart; but more of that later.

Back to the Kaiserhof. It was 13.50, and to my consternation I found Raeder already there. 'Oh, Großadmiral, you here already?' In my confusion I couldn't think of anything else to say. 'Yes, yes, I am the host, after all. But you . . .' at that he looked curiously at me and sniffed, 'you're dressed very soberly today.' 'As a Staff Officer, I need to become more serious, Herr Großadmiral.' 'But not too serious, please,' laughed Raeder, and brought to the proceedings a touch of humour which stayed with us throughout the following breakfast with the naval staff. When we broke up, the OdM (Oberbefehlshaber der Marine – Commander-in-Chief of the Navy) confided to me that he had awarded me the Crossed Swords; it had had to be ordered specially, and was still being made up.

Kapitän von Puttkamer, the Führer's adjutant, told me that Hitler wanted to decorate me with the Swords himself the following day in the Chancellery. So this time no Jockey Bar but an alcohol-free night at the Adlon. One shouldn't push one's luck. In the evening to my surprise Erich Topp called me up.

Suhren is awarded his Crossed Swords after his final patrol.

After he'd been taken off patrols he had become Chief of Tactical Submarine Flotillas in Gotenhafen, a classroom unit. At that moment he was on holiday in Obersalzberg, at Berchtesgaden, Hitler's retreat. He was actually staying in the Platterhof, which was an exclusive inn for invited guests.

My end of the phone conversation went something like this:–

> 'Well now; tell me, Erich, are you just ringing me up to congratulate me? In which case, let me reciprocate . . .'
> 'Ah, what do you mean, "Come on up"? . . .'
> 'Well, you may have got an invitation from Reichsleiter Bormann, but I haven't . . .'
> 'What do you mean, "Come up anyway"? . . .'
> 'It's all very well for you to suggest it, but you don't know that. Are you getting bored up there on your own?'
> 'What, you are allowed to bring a girlfriend? . . .'
> 'Yours has gone? Well, you can never rely on women . . .'
> 'Well, I'll see what I can do about "coming up" . . .'
> 'Cheers for now, then . . .'

I was certainly keen to do so, but to bring a girlfriend? How could I get hold of one short of stealing one? Apart from my occasional visits to the Scheherezade, nothing doing. I wasn't engaged or anything; we were always away at sea, and I had as a rule neither time nor opportunity for a girl even to smile at me. But every rule is made to be broken. Over a long period I had grown very friendly with the daughter of General G—-, whose son had been my 2WO. But as things were with us submariners, I was in no position to embark on a long-term relationship with the young lady. I had had a long discussion about it with my friend Hein; there were enough widows already. As I've already said, that was no longer an option.

The following day I reported to the cheery von Puttkamer. The Reich Chancellery was swarming with all the senior members of the Party: Abschnittsleiters, Gauleiters, Reichsleiters and what have you. Nothing but brown shirts everywhere. It was the day after the big 'Winterhilfe' speech, Hitler's charity appeal to the nation. Even as a sailor one would have had to be very arrogant not to be impressed by it all.

The formalities got under way. In front of me in the queue was Field Marshal Rommel, who had been fighting in Africa. No one could have guessed then that only two years later he was to kill himself – at the command of the same Führer who was now awarding him not poison but the Oak Leaves with Diamonds. While they were still talking together inside, the door opened and the marshal's baton and the decoration were passed out for von Puttkamer to hold. So I had the pleasure of inspecting both at close quarters, asked for the baton, and just for fun saluted those present with Rommel's status symbol.

I was very impressed with his Oak Leaves. It's true that I had one myself, but this was a very special one. Three diamonds in the middle of about one karat each were each flanked with two of three-quarter carats. The whole was underlaid with an oak-leaf of white gold or platinum. It constituted a personal present from Adolf Hitler to Field Marshal Rommel – mind you, from the same Führer who after 20 July 1944 offered Rommel the choice of committing suicide and having a state funeral as an alternative to being tried with the rest of them by the People's Court for high treason.

Then I was called in and greeted like an old friend. A colleague of Hitler's personal photographer, Prof. Hoffmann, took the customary photo of us shaking hands, and the Führer went to sit at his writing desk across the table from me. Hitler could be very charming when he felt it was called for. He sniffed out, so to speak, who he had in front of him. If he had just talked a load of waffle, it would definitely have gone in at one ear and out of the other. But I had the impression that he was being frank and truthful, and didn't feel that he had to be too careful about what he was saying, so I still remember our conversation very well. Basically he wanted to sound me out,

Rommel, decorated after his North Africa campaign.

as a young combatant, and see what hope I held for the submarine service. He could have got this sort of information from more senior officers than me, but perhaps he'd been told that I usually gave a straight answer.

His principal question was: 'Do you believe the submarine service can maintain and even increase the numbers of ships it is sinking?' Now the German submarines during the second half of 1942 were at the pinnacle of their success, and by that time had sunk three million tons. I voiced my reservations. 'Mein Führer, if thirty submarines can be built per month in the near future as planned, I believe one can be confident that the submarine service can sustain and possibly increase the rate at which it is sinking ships. The problem is that a single boat can no longer achieve the results that it could from the beginning of the war up to now.'

Hitler fired back the short question – 'Why do you say that?' 'The enemy, I am quite convinced, has radar in its planes. That means he can detect us much earlier; trying to get ahead of a convoy by day is getting very difficult, and it just about rules out the sort of surface attacks by night that we have made up to now.' 'Can't you defend yourself against planes?' 'It not as easy as that. The 2cm gun rusts up after a sea-journey of only a few days, and however much we grease it, it jams after only a few shots. I have no faith in the thing.' Hitler reacted as quick as lightning and jumped to his feet. 'Von Puttkamer, get Speer back at once. In that case the submarines must be fitted with rustproof guns.' While the Admiral went off to track him down, I made some more comments. 'Mein Führer, supposing the 2cm gun could be fired without any problems, if I have a plane flying over me, I don't have a stable platform from which to fire at it. Apart from that, as soon as the enemy realises that we intend fighting regular duels with them on the surface, he will just get a bigger calibre gun in his planes and shoot from a safer distance. Furthermore, I believe that in the future boats will spend more time underwater and less on the surface.'

So that was that. In the meantime, Kapitän von Puttkamer came back and said that he couldn't find a trace of Speer. I had a feeling that the armaments minister was all too familiar with the instant decisions of his master, and sometimes made himself scarce so that he couldn't be contacted. Hitler then spoke rather pathetically, rolling his 'r's: 'Herr Kapitän, if the submarines don't manage to sustain or increase their totals of sinkings, then the Allies will finally set foot on the European mainland; then Germany will have some dark days to go through.'

I was dismissed, with best wishes for the future. I left the hall with the order of the Crossed Swords in my hand. Instead of the expected two or three minutes, the whole thing had taken twenty-two; protocol had collapsed. I had been thinking back to our former meeting on the battleship *Tirpitz*, when Hitler had been the only one to open his mouth, and had been entirely unprepared for this longer dialogue with the most powerful man in the Reich. I couldn't help being fascinated by him; indeed he was in the habit of casting his spell over a wide variety of people. There was one impression that I gained, though; Hitler was no 'man of the sea'. The navy remained something quite foreign to his nature, however much they tried to keep him informed about it, and he found the submarines a bit of a mystery. In the past this had made it difficult for the BdU to push through its demands. On the other hand both Party and State left us in peace. And this was no bad thing.

The call from Topp was still on my mind, and at the cold buffet in the Reich Chancellery I asked von Puttkamer whether perhaps he could help me to get an invitation to Obersalzberg. I could see from his doubtful expression that he didn't hold out much hope of getting the Propaganda Minister to arrange this sort of invitation. 'Herr Kapitän', I said, 'Topp's been invited by Bormann. The Reichsleiter is sure to show up here; perhaps you could be kind enough to introduce me to him.' The good-natured 'Puma', as von Puttkamer was known among us, got on with the job straight away. 'Certainly – here he is now!' And, turning to Bormann, 'Herr Reichsleiter, may I introduce to you Teddy Suhren; he's just been awarded the Crossed Swords to his Oak Leaves'.

The stocky forty-year-old Minister, Hitler's secretary and Party Leader, was in fact a man much feared by his colleagues. Just now he was in a jolly mood. 'Congratulations! . . .' and so on and so forth. I took a deep breath and launched off; cheek won the day. 'Thank you very much, Herr Reichsleiter, – and especially for the invitation to Obersalzberg!' If Bormann felt surprised, he managed to conceal it. Very likely he was thinking about something entirely different. 'No problem; no need to thank me,' he exclaimed obligingly, 'only too delighted. My kitchen and cellar are at your disposal.' The Kapitän's hair stood on end with alarm. He quickly recovered, and warned me under his breath, 'My God, Suhren, that could have gone badly wrong.' I stayed calm. 'Of course it could; but as you very well know, in a submarine attack one's used to running the gauntlet . . .' 'Yes, but come on, . . .' I made an appropriate hand gesture. 'My kitchen and cellar are at your disposal.' Von Puttkamer shook his head forbearingly, but went on to make all the necessary arrangements. He was used to a rather different way of going about things in that place.

Erich Topp was waiting for me in Munich. A car took us to Obersalzberg. Obersalzberg, next to Berchtesgaden, was Adolf Hitler's special retreat, fenced off and well guarded. The individual buildings lay spread out over the area: the Berghof, the earlier Haus Wachenfels (Hitler's private quarters), the farm buildings, the SS guardhouse, the Platterhof, and the rest of it. It was all set against the wonderful backdrop of the Bavarian Alpine landscape. Bormann's model farm house was there too. A rural jewel of Southern Germany. In the Platterhof, the hotel of the top party leaders, everyone was lined up, from the manager to the youngest page-boy, and I was welcomed with the grandeur that only experienced hoteliers can summon up. So much fuss about my person was rather embarrassing. 'Kitchen and cellar stood open.' It was also noted with regret that I had come unaccompanied. Since Topp had also travelled alone, we were given two single rooms linked by a bathroom which lay between them. Very practical for snoring couples as well as for couples who didn't want it to be too obvious that they were together. They had thought of everything here.

And we found everything laid on. Germany of course was not starving, although food was rationed. But here people could still eat in the third year of the war as though in the middle of peacetime. We had no idea where the other hotel guests came from. They too could live off the fat of the land, only with the difference that they had been invited as paying customers. One of the staff was Josepha, the housekeeper of the guesthouse, who always managed to deal with whatever arose in her own particular common-sense way.

The goal of one of our expeditions was Salzburg. This was the first time I driven a Volkswagen, which was laid on for us, and I was impressed by the performance tucked away in the little machine. One night there, with Gauleiter Scheel, we met two cheerful sisters from the ski resort of Lech am Arlberg. Various colleagues of ours, including the unforgettable Mützelburg, had taken skiing holidays there, and with these friends in common we soon got on very well indeed. Scheel moreover remembered my sister well; she had studied architecture at Dresden while he was there. She had once been his partner at dinner and had taken him by the arm in a friendly way. That had greatly impressed Scheel; when he had been a student leader he had been accustomed only to credulous subservience or blind loyalty. So we all soon became a jolly party together, and even stayed overnight in the lovely town of the Archbishops, who, a good 300 years before, had driven the Protestants from house and hall alike.

Next day we were called back post-haste by an urgent SS order sent on Bormann's behalf. Bormann was the real master and organiser behind Obersalzberg; indeed if one is to believe the rumours the whole property was registered in his name. The Reichsleiter was waiting all ready for us in front of the Platterhof in a six-wheeled Mercedes. We were to go up to the Kehlsteinhaus, 1,800m up. This building was later earmarked as an Alpine fortress, built as it was on a rocky projection high over a sheer drop like an eagle's nest, but it didn't at all resemble an Alpine fort. It had been entirely Bormann's idea; when Hitler saw the whole thing for the first time, perched at such dizzy heights above the ground, he is supposed to have said, 'What the heck's the point of this monstrosity?' He had no great head for heights.

Our car made its way up the winding road cut into the cliff. Erich Topp, slim, fair-haired, and blue-eyed, the very image of a naval officer, sat of course beside Bormann, who was driving. I, being little Teddy, sat in the back. At a parking place high up everything came to a halt. In front of us a pair of double doors, and beyond that a tunnel through the mountain – the last 100m leading to the sanctuary. I never could resist playing with fire, and I commented, sounding casual, 'Well now, Herr Reichsleiter, please tell me, aren't these doors made of bronze?' 'But certainly; why do you ask?' 'Well, at a pinch you could always make a few torpedo tubes out of them.' Bormann laughed an ambiguous sort of laugh, and I felt that he wasn't too sure how to take my humble self. No doubt this powerful man, who by and large couldn't stand people having a joke at his expense, had clearly got other things on his mind. What matter if submarine folk shot off their big mouths? Give them jesters' licence, they'll soon be dead anyway.

At the end of the beautifully elaborate mountain tunnel, we travelled the last 10m up into the mountain on a chair-lift, and landed in Hitler's famous 'Tea-room' on the Kehlstein. The windows of the unique round tea-room gave magnificent views out over Watzmann and Königsee. One got the impression that Hitler's exceptionally thick walls were supposed to create a feeling of security in this high place. Mountain climbing wasn't exactly his strong point. It was on the tip of my tongue

Hitler's retreat at Obersalzberg.

to draw a comparison with the masts of the *Gorch Fock*, but I kept my mouth shut.

Glasses of choice schnapps were laid out on a silver tray for our consumption. I didn't need asking twice. Even Erich Topp, who wasn't too bothered about alcoholic refreshments, joined in heartily. The arrival of the big-wigs brought our delightful idyll to an end. In came Frau Bormann, Professor Scholten and his wife. Scholten was the gynaecologist who had attended Frau Bormann at the birth of her children. Also with the group were the Braun sisters, Eva and Gretl, and a Frau Schneider. A rather formal conversation around the tea table ensued, until my friend Erich happened to ask his neighbour on his right-hand side, who was Eva Braun, how she was serving the Führer in Obersalzberg. Blonde Eva came from the Hoffmann Studios and sometimes acted as hostess, sometimes functioned as housekeeper. Among others things she decided

Eva Braun, Hitler's eventual bride.

the menus, which had to be chosen to suit Adolf who was vegetarian. Otherwise she apparently had no fixed 'job', so it was better not to enquire too closely.

I tried hard to distract Erich, kicked him on the shins, and when that didn't do the trick, tried 'Erich, pass the biscuits over, will you?', and suchlike manoeuvres. Topp meanwhile stuck to his guns and persevered, to the quiet amusement of the whole company, who hid behind obviously unimportant small-talk. Even Bormann seemed amused. In all events I was relieved when the conversation finally took another turn, though I was sure the others had enjoyed watching Eva taking evasive action for a while. For all that, she had charm, was likeable, and wasn't angry with the young seaman. Frau Bormann invited us to supper at their house. We asked for time to change first, which Bormann granted on one condition – 'Only ten minutes though, gentlemen!' Once on our own again, I asked Erich whether he really had never heard the name of Eva Braun. He hadn't, why should he have? I had of course heard of her already. 'So didn't you realise that Eva Braun is Adolf's girlfriend?' To my amazement Topp said candidly, 'I did wonder about that.' 'Well, in that case you could have saved yourself a lot of questions!'

There was obviously some ulterior motive for the dinner-invitation. The Reichsleiter clearly wanted to sound us out about something or other. He was Chief of Staff, Hitler's 'grey eminence', who supervised everything, and who did everything to keep anything unpleasant at arms' length from his master. At the Bormanns' the whole group from the tea party met up again, apart from the blonde Eva. The many Bormann children had already eaten. The house was well but simply furnished, without any ostentation. Solid furniture, proper carpets, pictures of the master of the house: nothing over-elaborate. I had a raging thirst and was given a beer. As for the rest, the master of the house didn't leave us in the dark long about his purpose. Between cold sips he confided to us as though making casual conversation that Großadmiral Raeder had expressed a desire to be relieved of his position; who would we recommend as his successor? Just at that time we had suspected for a while that things were no longer going as they should have because of disagreements over naval strategy. Things had gone seriously wrong. As far as a successor went, we didn't need long to make up our minds. Topp spoke for us both, and I agreed with him: 'The war in the Atlantic can only be won by the Submarine service. Therefore it is logical that the man who built it up should also have command of the whole navy – and that at the moment means Admiral Karl Dönitz'. As far as we were concerned there could be no question of anyone else. That was the end of the matter. Afterwards, we had the impression that everything had been decided long before, and that Bormann only wanted to hear us reinforce his own preconceived opinion. And as everyone knows, that was exactly how things turned out. After Hitler and Raeder started coming to blows over the battleships, which were increasingly isolated,

Raeder was finally replaced by Dönitz in January 1943. Dönitz became Großadmiral.

Meanwhile the Braun sisters had turned up. With help of some good wine the atmosphere warmed up, records were chosen, and we started dancing. Carried away with alcoholic jollity I approached Eva with the words – 'Gracious madam, might I be permitted to dance the Submarine Swing with you?' Gretl Braun found a suitable record in the very varied collection, and Eva and I let our hair down with a boogie-woogie on the carpet. Both record and dance contravened all the rules of the Third Reich, since the minister for Education and Propaganda, Dr Goebbels, had banned these 'un-Germanic' dances. That of course only affected the ordinary people, not the top 10,000. Even Bormann raised his glass to me in a friendly way; 'Suhren, you're becoming more likeable by the hour!'

Without question Bormann was not a man with whom, shall we say, one could be particularly good friends. Many of his own associates found it difficult to relax with him, and it was said that even Eva Braun didn't especially like him. He gave off a disquieting sense of being tense and wary. I felt uneasy in his presence and tried extra hard to overcome this. But I felt that once his tongue relaxed with the alcohol he managed as far as I was concerned to shed that mistrust that had become second nature to him. In contrast to the mass of favour-seekers and opportunists for whom he had constantly to be on the look-out, we seamen weren't trying to get anything from him.

At midnight the Reichsleiter took French leave, and we intended to be off likewise. Frau Bormann, very quiet and ladylike, forbade this and insisted that we stay: 'I would be a poor wife if I couldn't deputise for my husband!' She seemed to take it for granted that seamen could put quite a bit away. So eventually it was 2 in the morning before we all got under way. Outside someone demanded 'A song!' So we sang the song 'Blue Dragoon' as we all – that is, the Scholtens, Frau Schneider, the Braun sisters, Topp and I – steered a course through the starry night to the inn where they happily let us in and we could carry on the party. Certainly, kitchen and cellar were at our service.

Eva Braun's behaviour was open and spontaneous. She appeared to enjoy having the chance to be herself for once: just a cheerful young woman, whom we treated as such. That was something we submariners were pretty good at. I'm sure she didn't often have such an unrestrained company around her. We had a ball and felt like kings of the sea. We finally called 'Diving Stations' at 4am. Later we heard from the head of the guard at Obersalzberg that he'd called up the guardhouse about the nocturnal warbling, only to be given the laconic answer – 'The Captains are in town!'

One more word about Josepha. Frau Josepha's job was to be housekeeper to the guesthouses. As I have already mentioned, she was a down-to-earth person who observed a great deal from behind the scenes and could tell many a humorous tale about it. She spoke of Eva Braun with great insight. 'What is the good of her having the most beautiful wardrobe tucked away, along with everything a woman could wish for, if she cannot be the wife of the man she loves?' On official occasions at Obersalzberg (which played no small role in politics) Eva had to make herself scarce. Her sister Gretl, who accompanied her most of the time, was better off. She didn't have the public image of a Hitler to worry about. Not long afterwards Gretl herself got married to Fegelein, the young Waffen-SS General and Obergruppenführer, who was Himmler's liaison officer at the Führer's HQ. Over good Bavarian beer at the Platterhof we tried to put the world to rights, and in the end I had to admit that it was all beyond me. It was beyond Erich Topp too. In order to distract ourselves we spent a boozy evening at Frau Weiss's bar at Hintersee.

The next day we were again invited to the Bormanns' for coffee. Along with the party already mentioned, Gauleiter Scheel appeared with the jolly skiing sisters from Lech. In addition he had brought with him Herta Feiler and Willi Fritsch, who had just finished shooting the film *Der Kleine Grenzverkehr*. I suspect there was a propaganda purpose behind it. Willi Fritsch behaved in the same relaxed way as in his films, and I found him easy to talk to. He wanted to be allowed to speak to his wife Dina Grace on the telephone, and I was able to get permission for this by asking Bormann on his behalf. When he came back he relayed greetings from his wife, who said she remembered our being partners at dinner on one occasion. I was pleased to receive her good wishes – even though her partner had been not me but my brother Gerd. Herta Feiler, who was married to Heinz Rühmann, gave the impression of being very stand-offish. I usually enjoy talking to beautiful women, but that wasn't the case with Herta Feiler. Did she always find it hard to relax, or was something about the atmosphere not to her liking?

The Reichsleiter, an experienced farmer, then came back to his farm, which was his hobby. From my own home-background I knew a bit about agriculture and cattle-breeding, so I didn't expect anything new, and had already used an excuse to get out of looking at it. But now Bormann got his own back; 'Ladies and Gentlemen, I would now like to show you our farm, – including you, Kapitän Suhren; you can't escape again this time!' What we were shown lived up to all the expectations one could have had – of a model. I expressed my 'admiration' rather coarsely to Willi Fritsch – 'All we need now is for the cow to shit on the parquet-flooring . . .'. Fritsch found my outspokenness a bit too risky, and moved a bit further away from me. At that point the party broke up quite cheerfully anyway. Scheel travelled back to Salzburg with his entourage, while Topp and I took ourselves off to Frau Josepha. She treated us splendidly to wine, beer and schnapps.

Overall, in the course of these three days I got on well with all of them, even the unpredictable Bormann. We had a lot of fun, but throughout all the familiarity managed to keep a proper distance. Indeed, as always, despite the pretence of 'One heart, one soul', there were also other overtones. In the

Suhren and Topp with Bormann's daughter Eike.

great German Reich the much-vaunted harmony between the Party, the People and the Services was not always in evidence, and one of these often tried to outdo the other. In exactly the same way the same thing was apparent here in miniature. It was clear that Scheel got on well with the film-people and the nice girls from Lech, and was completely ostracised by the others. I did my best to spread myself around equally between the two groups. Nevertheless, as they told me themselves, they felt here a bit like the musicians of Bremen – left out in the cold.

So this was our holiday in Obersalzberg and Salzburg, Mozart's town. The air was still full of violins, but the exuberant 'Submarine Swing' had been danced on the edge of a volcano. 1943 brought the defeat at Stalingrad, and Black May for the submarine service. And only two years later the short life of Eva Braun came to an end, poisoned by her own hand, even if she did at the last minute get married to Hitler. The husband of her sister Gretl, SS-Obergruppenführer Fegelein, was shot for treason on Hitler's orders the day before everything collapsed. After the death of his lord and master, Bormann is presumed to have perished in Berlin in the confusion of the last hours. He left behind a widow and a large number of children, and was sentenced to death in his absence at the Nuremberg trials. Obersalzberg fell into the hands of the Americans and souvenir hunters, and not one stone was left on another of the so-called Teahouse on the top of the Kehlstein, including the tunnel and the lift. In the words of Uhland, 'The guests in the Halls of Eden have vanished like dust' . . .

11

What do you mean, how many submarines have I got? – Attack on the green table – With 27th (Tactical) Flotilla – 'Boats to the Front, boats to the Front!'

My leave came to an end, and I had orders to report to Gotenhafen to begin duties with the 2nd Submarine Training Division (2ULD). But first I went to visit my parents. In Dresden it was suggested that I make a courtesy call on the Gauleiter of Saxony, Martin Mutschmann. I would need to prepare myself for the question, 'What do you make of the political situation?' Mutschmann greeted me in a broad Saxon accent that had to be heard to be believed. On of his first questions was indeed, 'What do you make of the political situation?' 'Well now, Herr Gauleiter,' I replied, trying to keep a straight face, 'I'm a submariner pure and simple; I've got all my time cut out worrying about the submarines.' 'Yes, now tell me, how many submarines have we got?' 'I could give you a figure, but it would only be approximate. On 1 January 1942 the Kriegsmarine had ninety-one submarines in all. After an intensive building programme, towards the end of the year there were at that time about 130 submarines in the Atlantic and another forty-eight elsewhere.' Mutschmann looked doubtfully at me. 'But surely we have more submarines than that?' I shook my head. 'I wish we did have more, Herr Gauleiter, but that's all we do have; and at the end of the day one has to apply the Rule of Thirds as well.' 'What do you mean, the Rule of Thirds?' 'That's how it works out: a third in dock for repairs, another third on their way out and back, and a third actually at the Front.'

The Gauleiter appeared exasperated. 'But surely every fighter pilot knows how many planes we have?' 'As I've already said, Herr Gauleiter, I can't discuss that – strict orders from the Führer, nothing I can do about it.' Then Mutschmann placed his hand on my arm, leant forwards and whispered confidentially, emphasising each word 'I'll just say this to you: you wouldn't believe what the Führer has got up his sleeve.'

Behind us lay three years of war. The wear and tear on hardware was beginning to show at the Front, a shortage of raw materials had set in, and there was a general lack of funds. Air raids were getting more frequent, and more and more problems were being experienced with producing submarines in the sort of numbers the Großadmiral was hoping for. Yet here sat the most senior political representative of the beautiful and hardworking province of Saxony who was trying to suggest to a baffled listener that Adolf Hitler only needed to put on his NSDAP cap and wave his hand to conjure up an assembly line full of guns, tanks and submarines – all the things that he had 'up his sleeve'. Afterwards I could only shake my head and wonder what on earth was going on. That's what they all thought: the Führer will sort it out, he's got everything under control.

The Kapitän of the 2nd Submarine Training Division was Kapitän zur See Hashagen, a famous Kommandant from the First World War, who had also written a book: *The Enemy in my Sights*. . . Once arrived in Gotenhafen, I also met up with my friend Korvettenkapitän Bleichrodt, who was my former Kommandant from *U-48*. He was now a wearer of the Oak Leaves and head of the training flotilla of little submarines known as 'canoes', in which future submariners took their first steps in the underwater world. In our delight at being reunited we steered a course straight for the wardroom, and I suggested that we ought to concoct a decent punch – a fruit-punch, of course. 'So, OK, how shall we make it?' 'No problem, Ajax,' I said, 'it's perfectly straightforward. A bottle of cognac as foundation, and to turn it into a fruit-punch add a bottle of cherry brandy and some more fruit schnapps on top

The *Wilhelm Gustloff* before the war as a Kraft durch Freude ('Strength through Joy') cruise liner.

of that. We can liven the whole thing up with a couple of bottles of champagne.'

We went ahead with the recipe, and started to drink it quite peacefully. To begin with it was all very civilised and business-like, but as time went on we kept on losing the thread more and more often. Overall though it turned into a fruitful exchange of views, ending with our resolve to train up what was now more or less the third generation of submariners, so that they would soon sort out the final victory. After we had pumped about two-thirds of the bowl dry, we set out on our way homeward. Bleichrodt lived on the *Wilhelm Gustloff*, and I had been given a cabin on the *Hansa*. After a few detours – and falling in once or twice – we made it to our target, where the Bootsmaat on duty and the deck watch spotted us and took us on board the accommodation ships.

I became a teacher and divisional officer of the trainee watch-officers, and gave instruction in tactics and naval warfare. It was a well-known fact that I had been brought in so that I could pass my experience on to the new boys; but I still hoped for a command at sea and not a job teaching theory in a classroom. Admiral von Friedeburg, of whom I thought so highly, must have been to blame for this, and it was typical of our relationship. He knew perfectly well that it was not my style, but still felt it appropriate to give me a temporary shore appointment. In the lecture room stood green ping-pong tables with grids painted on them. Model ships were moved around on them to simulate convoys, so as to demonstrate tactical manoeuvres. And that was where I found myself now face to face with between thirty and forty young Oberfähnrichs and Leutnants with little or no experience of the Front, myself being their staff-officer highly decorated with the Naval Sword of Honour. I had been awarded this in addition to the Oak Leaves with Crossed Swords. Later I realised that these trappings had been intended purely for propaganda effect. Clearly our mere appearance was supposed to be enough to stimulate the young men to do their duty. As an individual I seemed to be only half as valuable, though everyone was expecting me to make really rousing speeches. Now, I've never been one to use big words when little ones would do, and I'm no good as an orator. I had already warned them that I wasn't the teacher they took me for.

The end product sounded something like this: 'Now, gentlemen, you've all got a little red book like this. You need to read it through, and then you'll know how to drive a submarine. This is a first-rate naval handbook, brilliant for all peacetime conditions. Shut up and listen carefully. Now I shall tell you all you need to know about submarine patrols in wartime – and that is, attack! Everything else is of no importance; only attacking counts, attacking regardless of the circumstances. No attack, no success. Now then, you at the back, have you got that?' 'Yes, Herr Kapitän, – attack!'

I repeat, 'Attack! And that is why you will have to overcome your fear every time; it's no good if you cannot overcome your fear. I repeat that emphatically, since for the Kommandant on his own that continues to be the hardest thing; he's always got to tackle it afresh. And I tell you this, when you shortly get to the Front, whatever your thirst for action and your joy in attacking, you must all support your Kommandant; for he's quite capable of having an off-day too. Let me give you an example; up comes the radio-man with a report, convoy such and such. And while the Kommandant is considering, and having a hard think about it, you should simply go up to him all young and fresh and say, "I'll just go to the chart and help the navigator get the convoy's course marked down". That is how the Kommandant can be motivated to overcome his fears and get on with the job. Believe it or not, at moments like that I have often had to shove my knee into the metal of the bridge in order to get rid of the lump in my throat. So I repeat, you have to attack – go for the enemy, otherwise you won't be able to sink him. You there, on the left by the window, what do you need to do?' 'Attack, Herr Kapitän, attack!' 'Correct. Lesson over.'

It may be that my 'attack sermons' induced in them a deep psychological effect which extended to their freetime activities as well. As I have already mentioned we in the 2ULD were accommodated in ships as well as in staff-quarters and barracks. Among the former was the 21,000-ton passenger liner the *Hansa*, of the Hamburg-America line. This accommodation vessel had on board a supervisory officer as a sort of naval 'housemaster'; these were older men who had been put out to pasture. One day my young attack-happy submarine officers of the future caused a disturbance with their noisy festivities, to the point where the housemaster had to intervene and try to chase them back to their cabins. He hadn't taken into account the fact that he was in his nightshirt at that point, which turned the whole situation into a comedy and him into a laughing-stock.

When the course-leader came to my cabin on report as a result of the event, I gave him a wink and said, 'Open the door'. I lived on the same deck as the housemaster. Then I gave the course-leader a terrific dressing-down; where did he think he was, and was this a holiday-camp or the navy? As far as I was concerned I expected proper behaviour, and I expected him as course-leader to ensure that they put an end to such disturbances in the night – and so on and so forth. The housemaster in his cabin a few yards away could hear every word. Then, having gone through the formalities of tearing him off a strip, I gave him a wink – 'Close the door. Well now, he's happy. All that is by the by; you must realise that these old chaps are only doing their duty.' Next I apologised to the chap who'd been upset by the riotous behaviour of my pupils and took all the blame for it. So peace was restored once again.

The military kommandant of the district of Danzig and West Prussia had put out an order of the day instructing that only in exceptional cases should we be allowed to visit Danzig, Zoppot and the surrounding seaside resorts, and then only with a special permit. I didn't think this was fair. Why should all these splendid places be reserved for other branches of the services or for those stationed on the base? Was I supposed to be preventing people from enjoying themselves? 'No, Adjutant, you write out a special pass for all our course – yes, the whole lot of them. You'll all get a special pass from me for any town you want to go to. On one condition – that I expect you to behave yourselves, and not to get into any trouble; if any complaints get back to me I'll have to revoke all the special passes, quite apart from having to worry about the disciplinary consequences. And while we're about it', I said to them all on parade, 'I'd be grateful if you'd do me a favour. I don't like smoking on the street. If you're wearing uniform, a cigarette in the hand doesn't look good'. I didn't have to mention it again.

These young folks would shortly be leaving in a submarine, perhaps never to return. Why should they have to put up with these sort of restrictions of liberty in their last weeks of peace? They were all barely twenty years old; why should they need to be confined to a dump like Gotenhafen? I have to say that they didn't let me down; no one misbehaved. They were full of enthusiasm to get into battle, and were well and truly ready for action. In short, right through to the end we in the submarine service had an intake of men of a quality unequalled elsewhere, who continued to impress the enemy.

Politics affected us little; when at the end of January Großadmiral Raeder was replaced by Dönitz, even the change in the command of the navy passed almost unnoticed. Topp and I had already been expecting it since our conversation in Bormann's house. The new Großadmiral, who now left Paris and set up his headquarters in Berlin, had run the submarine service strictly single-handed. So we continued to operate more or less under the same regime. Nothing altered either as a result of our occasional meetings with the Party heads of Danzig and West Prussia. We were neither spied on nor provoked, though we expressed our views very freely to the officials. Perhaps they too thought, 'They can talk as much as they like: it'll all take care of itself. They'll be headed for Davy Jones' locker soon anyway . . .'. But we weren't given that impression.

However, another incident occurred. In order to sniff some country air – and horses – again, I made use of a free weekend to visit my old friend Hufnagel, from the horse farm at Stettin. A good deal else had been happening there. The German workers had all been conscripted, and the rebuilding was all in the hands of Polish prisoners and labourers. From their number they had formed a band of musicians, which in view of their talents was a remarkably good one. So Hufnagel said to me, 'Have a word with them, and see if they won't play the Polish National Anthem. It's a pretty tune, and the Poles are sure to enjoy playing it'. But the Poles were not at all happy about playing it. Under the given circumstances some felt it was going against the grain, and others felt it was a risky thing to do. At that I retorted, 'I am an officer and I take full responsibility. You don't need to blast it out, just play it nice and discreetly.' I was sorry for these men, who had lost their home between Germany and Russia in a war to which there seemed to be no end. They were very polite and friendly, like all people from country areas, and bore their sufferings with dignity. The tune had a very moving effect; 'Now is Poland no longer lost . . .'. The notes came out gently and almost dreamily. The instruments themselves seemed to sob, and tears ran down the cheeks of the players. No one could say a word afterwards, not even me. . . . But as chance would have it, one of the 100 per cent National Socialists spotted what was going on. Suddenly, from being a little pleasure that someone wanted to give to himself and a friend, the incident was blown up out of all proportions. 'Just imagine – to play the banned Polish National Anthem in the middle of the war.' A lot of lively letters were written off all over the place: and once again it all hinged on Teddy Suhren, who came out of it in the end with a black eye. Except that, once the grass had grown over the whole business, there was a surprising postscript to it. But more of this later . . .

My friend Erich Topp, who was like me a proud wearer of the Oak Leaves with Swords, was Chief of the 27th Flotilla. This was a training flotilla based at Gotenhafen. Its function was to prepare crews for the Front by practising convoy attacks using escorts and target ships. It was the last link in the chain that began with the models on the ping-pong table and finished with actual full-scale ships in the cold reality of the Baltic. From here the next step was the Front. Every ten days the flotilla was allocated new boats, so that Topp was always shifting from group to group without ever setting foot ashore. I had asked Erich to make a suggestion to von Friedeburg that I should join him as his assistant in the 27th Flotilla, since he could no longer cope with it on his own. With two of us we could relieve each other every ten days. So eventually I received a sea-going command again, and after my training course with 2ULD had run its course I became Gruppenführer and Chief of Staff with the 27th Flotilla in Gotenhafen. It was confirmed in writing on 13 March 1943.

So Topp sat on the submarine depot ship *Wilhelm Bauer*, and I travelled on the *Waldemar Kaphomel*. Behind us trailed a fleet of surface ships which were attached to the submarines for the purposes of the exercise. We did the best we could to ensure that the crews had the right attitude for going into action as well as the practical expertise they needed; but ten days was simply too short a time. Halfway through each course we would run into a little secluded spot to the east of Bornholm. Then we got the Kommandants onto our escort ship so that we, the two 'party-whips', could find out for ourselves whether they all were fully in command of their boat and had a good tactical grasp of how to attack a convoy. That was the moment of truth; no place there for nice words. The finger had to be laid on the wound, and it had to be made clear what needed to be brushed up. And there was plenty of that. Topp and I came across incredible instances of lack of knowledge and lack of ability in the young officers who were going to be the next sent off to the Front. It was the same with their crews.

The more boats we were sent the shorter we were of manpower. Von Friedeburg as the Admiral 2 I/C Submarines had the job of putting the crews together. He had to move fast. On *U-564* I still had a mixed crew – in other words a majority of old hands and a few new boys. But here, just about all of them were totally inexperienced men, mixed, if one was lucky, with just a few experienced hands – and that was the case right up to Kommandant. Topp and I, running our ten-day exercises in the Baltic turn and turn about, became more and more convinced that we should extend the training period to at least two months. What was the good of ten days? Kommandant and crew were altogether too green: but Dönitz needed the boats. That was where we differed. Our advice was, 'Better training, better training.' On the other side they demanded, 'Boats to the Front, boats to the Front!' It was already obvious how ill-prepared they were for it. To crown it all, these young lads got punished, incredible as it may sound, for their inexperience, something for which they could hardly be held responsible. At my first Kommandant's conference it came out that some of them had been punished by being put under arrest on board, having their leave curtailed, and so forth. One had rammed a pier, another had caused a dent, a third had broken a mooring-line, and another had got his position wrong. In my opinion to call these 'offences' was a bit much. In the interests of goodwill I declared the punishments to be unjustified and put a line through them all, provided they had occurred within the ten days of training. I had the authority to do that. I didn't consider it necessary to follow the practice of a certain Kiel flotilla-chief who had once said that they ought to be 'roasted' for every little offence – and that that was the easiest way to teach them their job. The word 'roasted' was unfortunately Kapitän zur See Sch—-'s favourite word, when he was in charge of submarine training. He was a man for whom otherwise I had the greatest respect. He always gave a coffee-party at the end of training, before the boats left for the Front. At it I made some remarks that were more or less critical of him. I stated clearly that it was not our job to punish these young and inexperienced Kommandants for the sort of trifling 'offences' which they couldn't help anyway. Whereat the exalted gentleman lapsed into an ominous silence. And sure enough, a few days later he rang up and said coldly that he had actually been waiting for me to apologise to him. I replied that if he felt he was being 'improperly attacked' – yes, 'improperly!' was his word – I would get in my car right away and come and visit him in his house at Zoppot. That I did without more ado. I managed to convince him face to face that we shouldn't be punishing these young Kommandants, but instead had a duty to be helpful to them all along the line. Every hour, every day, at every opportunity. These young people, after all, had a shrewd suspicion what was in store for them, and how difficult and dangerous their task was. They went off to the Front with the stoicism borne of inevitability – even though, to date, every third man had failed to return.

Altogether by the end of 1942 our submarines had sunk close on twelve million tons of enemy merchant shipping. 1943, too, was successful at first. For example the first three weeks of March alone brought in 500,000 tons. However, in April things suddenly fell apart. The enemy had been working on their defence systems for a while, and these suddenly became so effective that the submarines could hardly get near the convoys. At the beginning of the year the disaster of Stalingrad had heralded a turning point in the war on land; there was a similar set-back in the war at sea during so-called 'Black May', in the course of which one or two submarines went missing every day. On the 19th there were actually four, and the full number of losses for May reached the record total of forty-three. In June our losses dropped back to seventeen boats, but in July there were thirty-seven again, and we still couldn't discover in every case exactly what were the precise causes of these unexpected losses.

And so it went on.

In the training units we were not officially given the loss figures. We only found out through our friends and contemporaries on Dönitz's staff. We also knew which boats hadn't come back, so it was all pretty obvious anyway. This was the cue for Topp and I to rack our brains about how we could improve the training. We concentrated more and more on the 'Ten Commandments', but it was clear that the basic problem was that the whole training process for submariners needed to last not three but five months, if not actually twice as long. And even that was only half the length of time that had been spent on training in the 'good old days'. But after Black May submarine building, which had already been stepped up, was increased yet further from thirty a month to forty – at least on paper – and the crews had to be 'pushed through', so to speak, to make up for the losses. The cry was 'Boats to the Front, boats to the Front!'

We were determined however not to give up without a struggle, and to make our views known to Dönitz by word of mouth. And the question arose as to which of us should pay a call on the then supreme commander of the Navy. I thought we ought to decide who should go by tossing a coin. Topp could take tails and I'd go for heads, and we would see who won. It was my unspoken opinion that our self-appointed mission would just be a waste of time – if anything it was likely to rebound on us. It was obvious that Dönitz must have had the same worries, and wouldn't want to be swamped by all our complaints as well. But Topp insisted on going in the end. He was after all the senior officer, and he set off for Berlin. I could only warn him, 'Erich, Erich, I hope you won't regret this.'

Well, Topp went to Dönitz, but he didn't get much of a hearing, and didn't even get as far as mentioning our joint suggestions for improving training. He was told among other things that the convoy situation in the Atlantic was changing anyway: that the American Liberty boats and Victory ships, which were at that time being produced in such large numbers, were feeble things and badly built, so that they would have to be overhauled after their first voyage, the Allied docks would soon be overwhelmed by repair work, the transport of war materials would dwindle away, and the Allies would then run short of more than just merchant ships. Topp and I were staggered at such a naïve calculation, which had clearly originated

The *William T Shermann*, here part of an Atlantic convoy, was one of the many 'Liberty Ships', one of which could be built in as little as four and a half days.

from Goebbels' Propaganda Ministry. In fact, despite the way in which they were ridiculed, these mass-produced ships could still be found in every ocean some twenty or more years later under a variety of flags.

I'm quite sure that Dönitz himself didn't attach any significance to this sort of shabby pronouncement. He must have been able to see through it all, but wasn't allowed to admit it. For example, a colleague who had been on the sunken auxiliary cruiser *Atlantis* as adjutant to Kapitän zur See Rogge told us how Rogge had been to thank Dönitz for the rescue of his crew by submarines. During the rescue, quite out of the blue they had found themselves being attacked by the enemy. Rogge then commented to the BdU that they must have cracked our code. At that Dönitz, so my friend told me with dismay, became absolutely furious. I reassured him. 'You need to understand that Dönitz no doubt has the same suspicions, but as supreme commander it would not do for him to voice them. That would be bad for the morale of the troops. If our code is not supposed to be broken, then it cannot have been!' Dönitz had been ordered by Hitler to carry on the submarine war no matter what happened, in order to tie up the enemy's forces in the West. According to British sources, at that time more than 1,000 planes were kept busy by the submarine campaign. And if what I heard after the war was true, the ratio of forces at sea was 1:20 – in other words, twenty enemy ships were involved in trying to destroy each German submarine. Hence also the declaration by the 'GRÖFAZ', the 'Greatest Commander of All Time', 'The Atlantic is my Western Front.' So, our recommendation to 'Give them better training!' continued to contrast with 'Quick, quick, boats to the Front, boats to the Front!'

Whether we would really have solved much by extending the training-period for submarine crews is another matter. The enemy's defence systems, which had lagged behind for years, had finally and conclusively caught up with our technology – indeed had overtaken it. The hole over the Atlantic, known as the 'Gap', was now closed. There were no longer any areas of safety, any spots which we could relax in without being disturbed. On the one hand the aircraft possessed longer ranges which now covered the 'Gap', and on the other the enemy now had an ample supply of aircraft carriers available. And accompanied by submarine hunter-killers and escort groups they drove our boats under water. The planes themselves were equipped with radar, and could locate us on short wave, without our 'Metox' and 'Naxos' radar-equipment knowing anything about it before they buzzed us. In the Atlantic we felt as though we were surrounded by direction-finding stations; we could be located from great distances as a consequence of sending out even a short radio-signal. We knew virtually nothing about the nature of this equipment. 'Huff-Duff', the short-wave direction finder, as well as the new attack weapons and all that went with them – all that was a closed book to us and remained so right up to the end, while they continued to track us down. As experienced kommandants we were also well aware that our boats themselves were now pretty old. They were not designed to be proper 'submarines' at all, only 'submersibles'. Because of the limited supply of fresh air and the tiny battery capacity, both of which needed continuously to be replenished, their diving times were limited. Naturally they had been able to avoid being seen for a while, but only in the first phase of the war, when the enemy was dependant on asdic for locating us underwater by sound. That only worked if a submarine was known to be close; one could hardly probe the entire ocean with it. Our comparative invulnerability came to an end in 1942, when they became able to track us down by night and through fog. With an underwater speed of a mere 6 knots it made it very difficult for us to escape; we were always at a disadvantage when up against fast pursuit boats. That was the reason why the battle group in the Atlantic, on that particular occasion, got away literally from under my nose before I could fire a shot.

So that is how things were. Though we were caught in a cleft stick, we had to fight on. It wasn't always easy to show a confident face to the outside world. In the course of one of his periodic inspection visits the Großadmiral called on us and came on board the *Waldemar Kaphomel* with me. During lunch together, the ship's band added some spice to our simple meal with some lively tunes, and played amongst other things a naval march. Dönitz, who loved music, asked, as was his habit, 'What's the name of that march?' He got a wide range of answers: the Hohenfriedburger, the March of the Prussian Grenadiers, the March of the 18th Hussars, Hoch Heidecksburg! No good; standards of musical appreciation at sea are not usually of the highest . . . Finally it came to my turn. 'Suhren, what's that march?' I answered, distinctly gloomily, 'Herr Großadmiral, there's only one march I know about, and that's "From darkness to light" . . .' Dönitz was startled. My friend von Friedeburg was also there, and he got the message right away. Sitting at the next table he turned round and said over his shoulder, 'Suhren, the English have forgotten something; they should have shut your trap long ago!'

12

Führer of Submarines (Norway) – Jutta-Beatrix and the mother-in-law – HQ Narvik – Cowardice in the face of the enemy?

THE MILITARY SITUATION HAD visibly deteriorated. The Eastern Front was in retreat, and to the South the Allies had already set foot on the Italian mainland. The submarine service continued to be run with a view to trying to prevent a debacle at sea. The result was a change in tactics, and even though the U-boats' success rate had clearly dropped, at least there was no repeat of the high losses of 'Black May'. Periodically von Friedeburg came across from Kiel to Danzig and Gotenhafen to check up on the training situation there. On one such visit, early in 1944 he confided to me quite unexpectedly, 'Look, Suhren, the Großadmiral has decided to make you Führer of U-boats (FdU) in Norway. To be quite honest, I didn't go along with him. But the Großadmiral insists, so there's no point in arguing.'

These 'FdUs' were the long arm of the submarine directorate. The Großadmiral, who was still BdU, directed operations from Berlin, but under him, in three outposts as it were, there were three commanders of submarine operations, or Führers of U-boats: for the Atlantic, FdU (West) in Angers on the French coast; for the Mediterranean, an FdU in Toulon; and for the North Sea and the Arctic FdU (Norway) with his headquarters in Narvik. My promotion to such a high position surprised me, and gave me some misgivings too, for I was no longer convinced of final victory; in such a post I would be expected to give encouragement to troops spread over ten degrees of latitude, from Bergen to Hammerfest. Admiral Godt, chief of staff of the BdU, could give me no other advice than that we fight and keep on fighting. In the words of the proverb, 'If you're riding a tiger, it's not a good idea to jump off'; and you can't argue with that.

Von Friedeburg had told me in his inimitable way what colleagues I would find up there in Narvik. 'There would be so and so there', he painted a glowing picture, and so on and so forth. But sadly when it came to it I discovered that there were also some people based there who were not particularly well-liked in the submarine service, and who had in consequence been banished beyond the Arctic Circle. Amongst others, one of my subordinates inevitably turned out to be a flotilla chief who had been my boss in 1938. It must have been a bitter pill to swallow for this staff-officer to find that one of his former Leutnants was now in command over him. I also looked forward to the future with trepidation because the various bosses and advisors under my command were without exception Fregattenkapitäns and senior ranks. It was particularly worrying since in my final briefing face to face with Dönitz he had urged me, 'Suhren, do a good job; we don't want you marching back here to the beat of muffled drums, do we?' With all this on my mind I got into the plane which was to take me to Oslo. On the way a radio-signal was handed to me that in one fell swoop made everything much easier. I had been promoted to Fregattenkapitän with effect from 1 June 1944; so I was now equal in rank to the rest of them.

My young bride stayed behind in Danzig. I had married Jutta-Beatrix nine months previously. During my time at sea only fleeting encounters had been possible; once a training officer I had had the opportunity to have a good look round the local girls. I had got to know Jutta-Beatrix through mutual friends, which is certainly an approved way of doing things, though it doesn't always guarantee a harmonious life together. My wife was still very young, just eighteen, and I was twenty-seven – which certainly was a factor that contributed towards

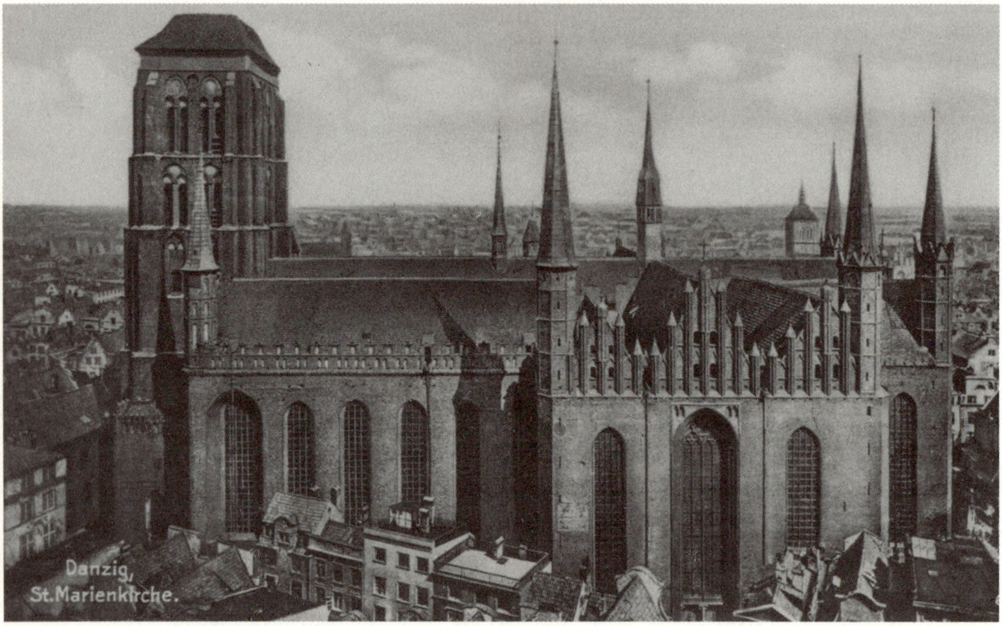

St Mary's Danzig, the church in which Suhren was married.

our going our separate ways later. The proverbial mother-in-law – just my luck! – put the lid on things. Her father was serving as an officer in the Luftwaffe on the Russian front. Her mother came from a family of dentists; and it was clear from her drilling questions that she regarded the Navy and especially her dear son-in-law with deep suspicion. The feeling was mutual.

Jutta and I were married in the beautiful old church of St Mary's in Danzig, in the presence of many relatives and friends. My submariner colleagues Bleichdrodt and Brandi were also there with their wives. I stood before the altar in full uniform, with frock-coat and sash, decked out with medal and ribbons, naval sword buckled on with the red-green eyes in its lion's head flashing, and everything was as festive as on a big flag-day parade. That was, until the parson opened his mouth. Then the festivities ground to a halt. I could hear my mother-in-law's words coming out of the parson's mouth. He started to reproach me for all kinds of things; apart from anything else he made it sound as if I treated my wife, young as she was, like a raw recruit. If they thought I was going to stand there and listen to this in silence, they had another thing coming. I lost my temper, and neither the sublime gothic of St Mary's, nor the illustrious congregation, nor the solemnity of the place and the occasion could prevent me from making my indignation felt. So I grasped my sword firmly in my left hand, took one step to the side off the red carpet, and banged three times with my weapon on the distinguished flagstones. The preacher hesitated for a moment, and gave me a terrified look. My friends could hardly control their laughter. Bleichrodt turned round and would happily have run out of the church. Well, to cut a long story short, my mother-in-law, in whose house we had ended up living, wasn't sorry to see me leave for Norway.

The head of the navy in Norway was the Commander, or 'Befehlshaber' (Norway). He was stationed at Oslo. On the coast were based three more naval commanders. In the southern section, (Bergen) was the much-loved 'Icke' Schrader, who was to shoot himself at the end of the war: in the central section (Trondheim) Schulte-Mönting, with whom I got on well: and in the north (Tromsö), hence next to Narvik, was Nordmann. These Admirals, who were unable to get a command at the Front or with a flotilla, I always imagined waiting for the invasion forces at the entrance to the fjords with machine pistols and anti-tank weapons. I got on the wrong side of Nordmann unintentionally in more or less the first few days. On the way back from Hammerfest to Narvik I passed through Tromsö, but didn't pay my respects to him. I had the opportunity to get on my way again quickly on board a minesweeper, which was then delayed for three or four hours due to circumstances beyond my control. Two days later the adjutant of the furious Befehlshaber (North) was on the phone complaining about the fact that I had failed to visit him. In order to get myself off the hook I promised to visit him at a convenient opportunity,

Schnee, Suhren and Ebell in Norway.

but with some mental reservations. Naval traditions were strong, but equally travelling around in Norway was a major problem. The plane had brought me from Kiel to Oslo, and the railway on from there to Trondheim. With me travelled Adalbert Schnee, who had undertaken missions in the North Sea and the Atlantic and on Dönitz's orders was to advise me up there. In Trondheim the railway came to an end, and we had to look around for some means of getting to Narvik. Schnee, who had already been there a few times, had a word with a friendly pilot who took us on from there – up hill and down dale – to our destination in his Ju 52.

The base was not in Narvik itself, where the Swedish railway terminated, but at Ankenäs, on the opposite side of the fjord that was surrounded by bare mountains. The command headquarters was the yacht named the *Grille*, which formerly had

German torpedo boats at Narvik.

been used for a number of state visits; and a Norwegian passenger steamer of 5,000 tons, the *Stella Polaris*, served as an accommodation vessel. Both of these ships, with their elegant clipper sterns, were rather out of keeping with the otherwise unexciting setting. In addition we were provided with ships which served as workshops and as stores – the *Neumark* (7,850 tons) and the *Huascaran* (6,950 tons), both manned by civilian personnel, as well as a civilian tanker. In Norway, unlike France, there were no submarine bunkers. Some of the boats lay near the *Stella Polaris* and some in the shipyard there, but most lay near the depot-ships.

Handing over the job took a while. My predecessor wasn't there any more. Our planes had crossed. When I talked to some of the staff at the base, the Chief of Staff asked me if he could be posted elsewhere. As things were, it couldn't have been easy for him; he would have been my senior as a Kapitänleutnant when I still ranked as a Leutnant. I would

Hitler's former motor-yacht, the *Grille*, Suhren's headquarters ship in Norway.

gladly have used my influence on his behalf, but I asked him to be patient for a month or two until I had sorted things out. Subsequently I was able to give him very much of a free hand, and soon sensed that he was beginning to enjoy his job again and had lost the feeling that he had been in some way demoted. The officer responsible for operations, Kapitänleutnant Reinhard Reche, held the Knight's Cross, was familiar with the North Sea, and was a thoughtful and quiet man. The officer in charge of administration, also a few years older, was similarly a great support to me. Equally the officers in charge of communications, weapons, and so on. I should make special mention of Engineer Officer Ebell, chief of the technical side, who later became a great friend. He was an exceptionally clever and ingenious organiser, who knew how to get hold of anything from a coffee-bean to a complete submarine. Whether or not they were older than me, they all helped me without reservation to do my job as FdU Norway – something that cannot be said for the rest of the Kriegsmarine. More of that later.

Under my command as FdU (Norway) were the 14th Submarine Flotilla in Narvik, the 13th in Trondheim, and the 11th in Bergen as well. There were supposed to be about three dozen boats on paper, but at most there were twenty-eight. In contrast to the FdU in France, who was guided in matters of strategy by Berlin, FdU (Norway) was expected to operate independently. This was something I had already come to realise. The most important aspect of my job was attacking the convoys which were taking war-materials by the northern route to the Russian port of Murmansk or were on their way back empty. Dönitz had initially put Korvettenkapitän Schnee with me in order to advise me on tactical procedures in the North Sea. But no sooner had we met up in Narvik than the Allies landed in Normandy. Adi Schnee packed his bags and flew back to Berlin. The Admirals had always expected a simultaneous landing in Norway, so I was requested to have my submarines standing by off the Lofoten Islands. I resisted this, being of the opinion that with their two fronts in France the Allies would have their hands full enough without coming over here as well. But if it were to happen, I made it clear that I would come down to Oslo with my boats and run things from there. So by order of the Naval High Command I had to send another five boats off to help counter the invasion. To my great regret they were lost; this could probably have been avoided had they remained in their own operational area, the North Sea and the Barents Sea. So we didn't have to wait long for repercussions as a result of my reluctance to send the boats to the Lofotens in readiness.

The operational area of my boats was not great. Roughly speaking it extended up to the North Cape and round the corner. But once they had fired their torpedoes and needed to replace them, or if they needed repairs and replacement parts, they kept having to go down to Trondheim or even to Bergen. That meant a wasted journey of 1,000km, and the same again to get back. This trip prevented them doing their proper job; they spent more time travelling backwards and forwards than they did in the actual war-zone. On the other hand in Narvik there were repair-ships that were not being used to capacity, with a special maintenance crew on board capable of carrying out work to the highest standards. In these floating workshops we later fitted six submarines with schnorkels (these were pipes which carried fresh air down to the boats when they were below the surface, and took the diesel exhaust gases away). These were completely successful, so you can see how skilled these civilian dockyard teams were.

I set to work right away to get better organised; in other words to improve Narvik to the point where 90 per cent of all requirements could be dealt with on the spot, and so do away with the wasted journey. That was easier said than done. The railway ended at Trondheim, and it was therefore inevitable that transferring parts, munitions, provisions and so on to Narvik could only take place by sea. But that required space in ships, and by 1944 tonnage was hard to come by. So I said to my engineer officer, 'Come with me to the Admiral (Norway), and let's tell him how impossible things are; they can't go on like this. We'll see what can be done about it.' I was quite optimistic because of the importance of the submarines, which had taken on the convoys and apart from the Luftwaffe were the only forces out there. But no chance; when I made my request in Oslo about a ship, the Admiral cut me short. 'Impossible, can't be done. I haven't got a spare ton.' 'But Herr Admiral, I must have this back-up. Somehow I have got to get torpedoes, parts, supplies and all the rest of it to Narvik to cut down the time wasted by the boats. They're spending too long travelling around out here, and are being prevented from carrying out their mission.' He waved me away; 'Nothing I can do about it. End of story; off you go!' 'OK, Herr Admiral,' I replied in my ever-hopeful but resolute way, 'in that case I'll have to make my own arrangements.' His chief of staff, also an Admiral, looked poisonously at me. He couldn't stand me; perhaps he'd been warned about me! Meantime I could hear Dönitz's parting words ringing in my ears – 'Make sure you do a good job.' Despite whatever objections they might raise, I had decided to challenge some of the highest ranks in the navy.

So I said to Ebell, 'Let's go to the Chief of the German Civil Administration.' That was Reichskommissar Josef Terboven, whom I had got to know when I arrived in Norway. Terboven was definitely a hard man, but he could appreciate the realities of the situation. And he wasn't very keen on the navy. He explained why; 'Großadmiral Raeder had recommended that I deal with Quisling. Nevertheless I would much rather work with the Norwegian parliament, Store Ting; this would be much better in the long run for German-Norwegian relations than working with the Nazi sympathiser Quisling.' Vidkun Quisling was an ambitious Norwegian politician and former war-minister who had collaborated with us from the start. Since 1942 he had been the leader of the national government. His name became synonymous with 'working for the enemy'. Terboven didn't think much of him, despite all the Navy's recommendations. 'What would you say if I came on board as a guest and started to tell you how to do your job?' Whereupon I answered, in so many words, 'Herr Reichskommissar, I'd kick you up the backside!' That was exactly what he wanted to hear. He laughed heartily; 'It's a pity I can't do that!'

Terboven listened attentively as I told him about my worries, and how I got no support from the navy. Then he called up his advisor on shipping. 'Kapitän Suhren needs some tonnage for Narvik, no strings attached. Can we let him have something?' 'Well now, let me see, I might just have a little coastal steamer.' I was delighted; 'That's marvellous! I could carry everything up there for myself and the boats.' 'Great', said Terboven, 'and if you ever need me to do you a favour again, I'll see what can be done.' Later, Terboven gave up. Every time he brought his problems to Hitler, he was bowed out – like Topp with Dönitz. When the end of the war was in sight, he gave me a call in Narvik. 'Suhren, come to Oslo, we'll have a fling again.' I refused, as politely as I could; my boats were in the middle of a desperate battle in the Arctic. When it was all over, Terboven committed suicide. Quisling was sentenced to death by his own countrymen, and executed in October 1945. Through my unauthorised dealings with the Reichskommissar I had incurred the displeasure of the Admiral (Norway), and became increasingly aware of that. What matter; at least I had my little steamer that ran back and forth between Trondheim and Narvik and kept us supplied with everything that Ebell procured – and Ebell could procure anything.

For the first time it became my job to send boats off into the war zone. The days of the big convoys were passed. The destruction of PQ 17, for instance, which was composed of thirty-five freighters from the USA, and had set off with the intention of travelling to Russia via a route north of Iceland: twenty-four of their ships had been lost, through the combined action of submarines and the Luftwaffe. This was no longer feasible. It was the end of 1944, and we were carrying on a dogged struggle against an enemy with a strong defence; they could lose themselves in the dark of the Polar night and make themselves invisible in the mists coming off the waters of the Arctic Sea. The ocean was infinitely large, and we never knew what detours the Allied freighters would make before setting their final course towards the port of Murmansk. Reconnaissance left a good deal to be desired. Over the telephone I asked the Director of the Airforce (Norway) about giving us the sort of support which we had been accustomed to getting in the west. The General's answer was discouraging; if there wasn't at least six- or seven-tenths cloud-cover, he wouldn't send any reconnaissance planes out over the North Sea. They would have hardly glimpsed a convoy, and if they had got close enough to see it they would have been shot down by anti-aircraft fire.

So I had to construct extended search-lines using the submarines themselves, and wait for a convoy to stumble into them. Sometimes radio signals, when deciphered, gave absolutely precise information about which ports an enemy convoy was leaving from, and its destination. In the case of the first convoy we didn't manage to make contact with it despite the length of the reconnaissance line. But we had information that a further convoy was headed for Murmansk. Fifteen boats lay ready for sea in Narvik. Using these boats as well as those which were already stationed in the area of operations I set up a long reconnaissance line all over again in the North Sea. I told the fifteen kommandants, 'Should the convoy get past us again without being spotted, I'll give you a code word which will tell you to head for Murmansk as fast as possible in complete radio silence. I give you a free hand to organise yourselves in whatever way you wish, as long as we catch the convoy.' In fact in the end I had to give the code word, since it became clear that the convoy had given us the slip again. On that occasion they ended up fighting a bitter battle with Soviet destroyers, British submarine chasers and convoy escorts. Some ships were sunk, and others so badly damaged that Soviet tugs had to tow them away or beach them. Sadly as well as successes we suffered losses. I was beginning to get a definite impression that the enemy was breaking our codes.

As FdU I was supposed as part of my duties to call on all the bases in Norway, and to give pep talks to the men. But just then convoy operations took precedence and I had to put off everything else, even visits to the sector Admirals. This earned me a black mark, and I had to apologise. There was enough to do in Narvik. The highly skilled staff of the workshop boats was working round the clock to keep the boats ready for action; if we didn't have some successes to show for it, the enthusiasm of these men, overstretched as they were, would inevitably wane. And personal contact and frank chats with the Kommandants as they came back from the Front meant more to me than formal visits to distant HQs. Kommandants were always a variable quantity. I had very good ones and less good ones. We are only human, and it is hard for us to avoid being influenced by personal feelings, by inclinations and subconscious prejudices.

We get on with one person well, with another less so. But as a commander one needs to stay impartial and to treat them all the same. No one should be able to spot whether he's a favourite of the commander, or the reverse. One Kommandant's character especially appealed to me. One day he said to me (these were his very words) 'Herr Kapitän, we're basically all under a death sentence.' I tried to talk him out of his gloomy state of mind, and urged him, 'Just watch out and think ahead; but I don't blame you for feeling you have to say this, nor do I see it as cowardice'. When the boat went to sea next, and glided past the *Grille*, its officers stood on the tower and saluted me. The Kommandant in spotless white cap, called out to me, in the words of the ancient gladiators, 'We who are about to die salute you!' And, God knows, he was right, too. They never came back. I found that hard.

Through Adi Schnee I had got to know the Naval Staff Doctor Dr Pantel, from the hospital at Narvik. Our casual acquaintance soon developed into a close bond between the two of us, which helped me greatly in my role as a very young Fregattenkapitän and Führer of Submarines (Norway). My talks with this surgeon I found to be really worthwhile; they both gave me advice and helped me to make up my mind. Dr Pantel was the only one to whom I could pour out my heart and whose opinion I could seek – as an outsider, as a doctor, as a decent human being. That meant a lot to me. One day my oldest staff officer told me that one of the Kommandants had confided to him that he felt psychologically incapable of having the courage to attack. In short he was a coward. Without making a great song and dance about it I tried in private to talk this Kommandant round. All he needed to do was to get control of himself at the first onset of nerves, and everything else would then follow of its own accord. He was very surprised, and had difficulty getting his head round what I was saying; in the course of our conversation I described how nervous I was before each attack – as I had already repeatedly told the pupils of the 2ULD. In his eyes I was a man who knew no fear. My God! I could only reassure him that in my experience there was no Kommandant, in fact no soldier at all, who hadn't had the jitters before every attack, wondering whether their number was about to come up or not. His fears therefore were absolutely normal. Before I sent this Kommandant off on a new mission I arranged a code-word with him. Should he find himself again in a dilemma and be unable to make decisions, he should transmit this code-word to me, and I would then call him straight back on some pretext or other. But the opposite happened. The Kommandant carried out an exemplary patrol, torpedoed two freighters and two destroyers and came back to Narvik bursting with pride. He was very taken aback when I told him that he had to come ashore because I needed him as chief of staff of a flotilla. He said of course – quite reasonably – that he had now got over his failings and would be very successful in the future. I wouldn't be moved. I knew from experience that this kind of Kommandant most probably wouldn't return from his next patrol. Just to prove the point to themselves and everyone else, they usually gambled the lot on a single card in a state of high elation: 'they can't get me!' I was delighted with his success. My words had fallen on fruitful ground. Such Kommandants, who were prepared to talk to me frankly and honestly about their lack of enthusiasm for an attack, were dearer to me than the others who falsified their War Diaries and in the end were denounced by their own men for cowardice in the face of the enemy.

That actually happened. I hadn't known the man in question very long, but I suspected something of the sort and hoped that I wouldn't have to get rid of him and put him in front of a court-martial. However when the facts were known, there was nothing else for it. Looking for things to say in his defence, I had a word with Dr Pantel: what could we do to play down his offence? We agreed that it just wasn't possible to turn every officer into a Kommandant as a matter of course just because he wore gold armbands. There would always be some officers among them who simply weren't up to the job. In the event of their failing to make the grade they would end up being court-martialled, so it would be better if for them to be put at the outset in a subordinate position where they would be happy to do a good job. I said, 'Pantel, you're right. Your task as a doctor is to preserve life. And what have I got to do? I have to keep on sending them off until eventually they're sunk. Every time a boat fails to return it makes me almost ill. I can't sleep from wondering what has happened to it.' Pantel asked for permission to declare this Kommandant sick. He would offer a plea to the court-martial along those lines. I asked him to do everything he could to protect this man from the harshest sentence of the military penal code – the death-penalty. And it came off; the accused man was demoted and got off with a few years of imprisonment. His successor – I couldn't believe my ears – was all of twenty-one years old. That made me realise how difficult it was for von Friedeburg to man all the new boats. The new lad did so well, against all expectations and despite his age, that I was able later to recommend him for a KC.

I've already mentioned that because of my unauthorised activities I didn't have the entire support of the naval command in Norway. Rumours of this may have reached the homeland, for on one occasion von Friedeburg commented privately to the Großadmiral that I'd gone out there like a bull in a china shop, instead of being prepared to compromise and trying to get on with everyone. So I asked him to pay me a visit sometime so that he could discover the extent of the problems the Norwegian base was causing for me. For example, the Admiral one day decided to take away my command-ship, the *Grille*, and transfer it to Oslo. The smart little ship with the colourful clipper stern had been in its heyday a flagship for the top brass, and was comfortably fitted out. Perhaps the people in Oslo were worried by the thought that I might be sleeping in Adolf's bunk. I replied to the order, 'Jawohl, Herr Admiral, right away, Sir . . .'; but I sent my radio-officer to Berlin and put in for a new and more powerful radio-transmitter. As expected, they dismissed us out of hand on the grounds that we had everything we needed on board the *Grille*, superbly equipped as it was with all the latest technology; it must therefore stay at Narvik. And that was the end of that. In my position as FdU (Norway) I had the support of the Großadmiral, so that I could act as I thought fit.

When I had to go in person on one occasion to Berlin, I told the BdU about my experiences, and about taking precautions in radio-traffic with the boats. Once again the enemy seemed to know our codes, though the German code-breakers had emphatically discounted such a possibility. This time the Großadmiral didn't contradict me. In fact both sides had known the opposite side's codes for quite a while and been able to look at each other's cards. It just demanded a considerable expenditure, and sometimes so much time that the encoded signal had already been overtaken by events and was no longer current. It was worthless unless one could go straight into action at the appropriate spot.

The Front drew ever closer to the borders of the Reich. As the war rolled like a ball ever faster towards the approaching precipice I once again took the opportunity to visit Danzig. I tried to persuade my wife with an emotional appeal; 'Pack your bags and get out, I've got digs for you in Allgaü.' My mother-in-law launched into a performance – 'Everything is quiet here; don't you read the Defence News?' I could only shake my head at this sort of naiveté, and shout, 'What the Defence News feeds us is just choice titbits – designed for idiots like you. I can only repeat, get out while you still have the chance before the Russians arrive. Or do you want to travel in winter – and with your little darling, too?' We really had a go at each other, anyway, I and the old girl who still believed in the final victory. After all, 'her husband was still in Brest-Litovsk' . . . So what? Her husband was indeed still in Brest-Litovsk, but not for much longer. He was sent to command an air base in Breslau. Good friends of his warned him that Breslau was cut off by the

Russians, and there was no point in his trying to get in there without being caught. But my father-in-law obeyed his orders to the letter, walked straight into a Russian prison camp and shortly afterwards died in hospital there.

That was later. I made another attempt, however, to persuade my wife with sensible arguments and urgent letters that it was high time to leave Danzig. But all the time my mother-in-law's influence held her back from doing so. Finally in the nick of time I called up the authorities and managed to get them to help with evacuating the two women. They finished up at Oberstdorf in Allgaü. After the surrender, as it happened, an American Officer's Mess was set up there, and when I turned up there some two years later, because of the restrictions placed on my freedom of movement, mother and daughter were both being well-looked after. I could leave again with confidence. Strange how life turns out.

13

Belated projects – Surrender – 'Missions Hotel' and imprisonment – The Warrior's Return

MY BROTHER GERD HAD MEANWHILE been promoted to Korvettenkapitän. He and Adalbert Schnee had been working for months on developing a new type of submarine and getting it ready for the Front so as to give us the upper hand again. It was the Type XXI, the so-called Electro-Boat. The Electro-Boat was a compromise between our elderly Type VIIC boats and the Walter Boat. Professor Walter from Kiel had invented an engine that could break down concentrated hydrogen-peroxide and use the resultant water and acid mixture as a propellant fuel for rockets, or to drive a steam engine: the Walter Turbine. With this means of propulsion the ideal submarine had arrived, which didn't depend on fresh air and didn't need to surface any more, and because of its shape and powerful engine could achieve a high speed under water. It was impossible to locate or to overtake. Its disadvantages were its high fuel consumption and the risk of explosion. For that reason the Walter engine never progressed beyond a couple of smaller trial boats.

But my friend Schnee had taken on the concept of the Walter-Boat, and though it hadn't been his design originally it was being developed more or less as the 'Schnee-Engine'. These new boats were designed to be able to approach a convoy at a speed of 25 knots under water, and fire off ten torpedoes at once, like a 'Stalin Organ', a sort of multiple rocket-launcher. These were target-seeking torpedoes, which reacted to sound and could twist and turn between the ships in a convoy. Our primitive old Type VIICs would then just have the job of picking off the stragglers. In principle that was all well and good, but it was one of the projects that came much too late to be realised.

Instead of these the Electro-Boat, the Type XXI, was developed, as I already mentioned. Its fish-shaped hull derived from the Walter-Boat was still, it is true, driven on the surface by diesels as before. However, its spacious diesel tanks were filled for the most part with electric batteries, which gave it a good turn of speed. The new boat, which had a schnorkel fitted as well, was named the 'Electro-boat'. One such boat was *U-2511*, on which Schnee and my brother served. Dönitz had brought the two of them together in the expectation that the two with the greatest experience of submarines would run the boat in quickly and get it to the point where it could be used at the Front. Schnee was delighted with the boat, I myself less so. Despite everything it took seven months for it to work through its teething troubles. On 1 May they finally left Bergen for the Front. The boat passed the test with flying colours. Its high underwater speed left all the groups of submarine hunters standing, it handled excellently, and it was impossible to detect, to the point where it managed to approach a British cruiser escorted by destroyers to within 500m without being noticed. Schnee's verdict: 'The boat is outstanding, both in attack and defence, something completely new for the submarine service.'

Still, it was all pointless. *U-2511* never again had an opportunity to shoot. On 4 May 1945 Dönitz had already given the cease-fire to the submarines. Having become Head of State after Hitler's suicide, he had immediately entered into armistice negotiations with the Allies, and unconditional surrender on all fronts followed shortly afterwards, on the night of 8/9 May. The British cruiser which Schnee had nearly caught in mid-patrol found itself immediately ordered to Bergen to supervise the surrender.

The German fleet was widely scattered at the time, and as part of the surrender process the Allies gave orders for them to meet at fixed 'collection-points' and to be handed over there. We in Narvik felt that we were situated a bit too close to Murmansk, and that the Soviets might decide to occupy Narvik and take us over too. As a precaution I appealed to Allied Command and suggested that as regards getting all the submarines together, we could bring them and all their attendant ships to Trondheim. The British agreed to this. It was a question of about fifteen submarines, the *Grille*, the accommodation vessel *Stella Polaris* and also the two repair ships and the tanker. So we left Narvik and headed south. Five British corvettes met us outside Trondheim to collect the submarines together; a few were following on behind, so that in the end about twenty turned up. Their intention was to whisk the lot away at once. In spite of all my on-the-spot objections there was of course nothing one could do about it. A rather arrogant English Lieutenant asked whether I wasn't aware that we had to follow Allied orders. So all my boats, which I had still been intending to deliver to Trondheim, were taken out of my hands and whisked off to England together with their crews. Our men still tried it on a bit over there, but the English told them to keep their hands off the engines, which were undamaged, and not to do any sabotage. The submarines surviving in German ports – about 150 in all – were not handed over, but were scuttled.

Of those that were taken to England a few were divided among the Allied navies, but the bulk of them (rather over 100) were taken out into the Atlantic soon after the surrender and were scuttled. This was the so-called 'Operation Deadlight'. The last word is the sort of cover one puts over a porthole to darken it; in landlubbers' terms, a window-blind. So the expression had a double-meaning; the blinds were drawn, the game was up.

There was no BdU any more. I had to make my own decisions about what to do next. When I arrived in Trondheim, I advised the chief of the flotilla (now minus his flotilla): 'Get all your people to clear everything out of the base and bring everything to our reserve stores'. These were tucked away in a hidden corner of the fjord. Submariners were always good at organising things. In no time they got hold of some trucks from the Luftwaffe. Everything that wasn't nailed down was packed up and carried off to the stores some distance away. Not a minute too soon. Scarcely had the last truck left the base when the Norwegian army arrived and took the whole place over – but they found the birds had flown and left an empty nest; not a bed, not a cupboard, not a desk, not a spanner, not a bolt. They weren't too happy about that. We pretended to be stupid; and the English weren't particularly interested – they were only bothered about the ships. Above all they wanted to keep the whip-hand, and not to hand things over to the Norwegian units which had appeared by now from somewhere or other. Who was actually in command (that is, was Senior Naval Officer in Charge), I personally had no idea. I dealt later with a Major Barnett, who was an interrogating officer.

I resigned myself to a longer stay, and had built for myself outside on the banks of the fjord a head office, containing a living room, a bedroom, a storage room and a shower – and fitted with a searchlight. For it was the wish of the Allies that I should continue as boss, and be responsible for the five store huts in which the rest of the submariners were accommodated, as well as for the compound of German prisoners who were under interrogation. They were in a barrack compound surrounded by barbed wire, a proper POW camp. It was still there, and what was more the Tommies had no intention of turning the inmates loose. On the contrary: the established regime was to continue. We submariners were commandeered as guards and given the task of maintaining order and discipline, if necessary by force of arms. That was a thankless task, and not without its problems; the offenders didn't want to be ordered about by anyone, no matter where they came from.

One day a few prisoners escaped onto Norwegian soil, which caused a bit of excitement. I explained the situation to the guards. Yes, it was said that they had dug their way out under the wire perimeter fence. Well, I gave orders to them to enforce a strict set of disciplinary measures; but one of the internees was eavesdropping in the next room and overheard the lot. Having nothing more urgent to do, he ran round the huts; 'Suhren has said so and so . . .'.

When I was due to leave, a racket started up behind me. I asked the camp leader, a young Kapitänleutnant, 'What's up now?' 'Well', he replied, 'it's directed at you.' Unarmed as I was, I got calmly out of the car, and roared, 'Back to your huts; come on, quick march!' This confident approach soon brought them to their senses. I quickly turned to the guards, and gave the order, 'Charge!' When the rabble-rousers saw that the guards meant business they dispersed bit by bit till eventually they were all back in their huts. I got hold of five burly NCOs from my own men. In the meantime another two had broken out of the POW compound and were making a nuisance of themselves in the area. The NCOs caught them, tied their arms and legs together and catapulted them back over the two-metre-high wire fence. Finally we got the biggest troublemakers out and brought them into the submariners' compound, where they couldn't get up to any tricks.

In due course it was my turn to be arrested by the English and put into Trondheim prison. This jolly building was called the 'Missions Hotel', and had seen better days. Recently the SD had installed themselves in it, and had set up eight cells in the basement. It was in one of these that I now sat. It was all over the question of whether I had once shipped five members of the Security Services up to northern Norway in a submarine. They had vanished without trace, presumably over the green line into Sweden. Our submarines had had plenty to do without that. There were also certain rumours flying around about my arranging to hand the *Grille* over to England. 'Yes, sure, listen, it was the FdU (Norway), Teddy Suhren himself,

U-564, under Suhren's successor Hans Fiedler, was sunk by aircraft in June 1943; a sketch from a survivor's account.

who had set the whole thing up. He would have done anything for the English in exchange for tea and cigarettes.' So for my own safety I had to be imprisoned right away, while the rumours were shown afterwards to be nothing but the usual denunciations. Then, quite unexpectedly, the Norwegian superintendent of the 'Missions Hotel' took my side. 'We're no better than you,' he said, 'we are making exactly the same mistakes that we have accused you of. We're missing the point. I shall shortly return to civilian life, and once I'm out, I'll make sure they free you. Really . . .'. I had the opportunity to celebrate Christmas 1945 with my submariners again.

Eventually something else cropped up to do with me. Off we went to the main prison in Oslo, to the fortress of Akershus. There I was given a cell on the top storey; I was the only prisoner on the whole floor. I wasn't clear why. It was pretty boring, apart from the interrogations, which were all talk and shouting; in the end even the novelty of these wore off. The Englishman with the loudest voice was undoubtedly a German. It was a joy to hear him speak so beautifully, and he had at his disposal a repertoire of swear-words which I'd

Suhren's prison in Oslo, the Akershus.

never heard before; and that's saying quite a bit. I didn't discover his rank, since he was dressed as a civilian; but he was without a doubt in charge of things, and everyone took notice of what he said. I said to myself, 'You'd better be straight with him' – which I managed to be, for I was never one to beat about the bush. And he saw to it that I was moved out of solitary confinement in a one-man cell, into a shared cell, which already held two colleagues. It felt like being back at the 'Missions Hotel'.

One of the two, an Oberleutnant in the Luftwaffe, asked me whether their morning 'exercises' would bother me. I shrugged and answered 'No problem as far as I'm concerned; do whatever you want, Yoga, breathing exercises, whatever'. But the other one was an older Feldwebel, a former member of the Security Services, one of the really keen ones. He had undergone a conversion since then. He had remembered that he was a Catholic and had become pious again. So now they held a service every morning. Why not? – only I didn't entirely get on with the Luftwaffe man. He kept trying to appeal to my conscience on the quiet. 'You know, Herr Suhren, we've all done something in life that we should really have been locked up for. Do you understand? I regard myself as having to sit here now and do penance for that; and I'm sorry for it – even if the 'Missions Hotel' wasn't particularly clean. God has brought me here through his great goodness.' 'Repent,' I replied, 'Repent? I'm afraid you and your philosophy aren't going to win any bouquets from me. I haven't committed any crimes, and I want to get out of here instead of doing penance, courtesy of the English.'

But I did go on my knees – to the man with the loud voice, who always seemed to me to have the last word. There were certain indications that he originated from very high-up in the German aristocracy. I know what I'm talking about. He managed as a result to get me put in an 'open cell'. As an inmate of an open cell one could move around freely within the prison grounds. What was more I shared this accommodation with the previous FdU (West), Kapitän Hans-Rudolf Rösing. He had made his way to Bergen with a submarine that had lost its Atlantic base after the invasion.

There I met all sorts of prisoners. Among them there were also a number of young men who had previously been some of the most loyal supporters of the Third Reich, but were now full of mutual recriminations – as is always the case, when things have gone badly wrong. They needed to be brought to their senses and to learn how to keep their mouths shut. The more they gave away about themselves, the longer they were kept there. They saw the point of that. I took part in discussions, and gave short talks on the submarine campaign and suchlike and in the end got into everyone's good books. And the men even said, quite spontaneously, 'If the English try to do anything to you, they'll have to deal with us first.' But the English weren't bothered about me.

One day in April 1946 Major Barnett and the civilian with the loud voice sent for me. 'Look at this German ID card. Is it a fake, or not?' I looked at the thing all ways up. It was as plain as a pikestaff that the document was a forgery. I shook my head and got out of it in my own way. 'Major Barnett, I have no idea whether this pass is genuine or not; it's a minesweeper ID card, and I'm a submariner!' And that was that. Whatever the motives for their question may have been, for some reason they seemed to respect me. The major and my exalted patron got to their feet and shook my hand in their typically English way. Perhaps they just wanted an excuse to see me again.

Shortly before that a letter had reached me – through all the checkers and censors – from my wife, to tell me that my sister and my parents had committed suicide to escape from being lynched by the mob.

The next day, suddenly, there it was: 'Suhren, come on, pack your bags!' The German military police fell in – they had kept their jobs too. The commander of all the German forces in Oslo, a Fregattenkapitän, had sent his adjutant; and the last Führer of Submarines in Norway left for Neustadt in Holstein.

I still had my few valuables: the Iron Cross, the Submarine Badge with Diamonds, the Knight's Cross, the Oak Leaves, the Crossed Swords; and the naval dagger of honour. I had put them all into a case that arrived in Copenhagen under the floorboards of an air-sea rescue boat. There one of my former staff-officers got it out and brought it over in a minesweeper that happened to be going to Kiel. That was where my brother Gerd was stationed with the German Minesweeping Administration, in Friedrichsort, and he took possession of the case. So in the end I got them all back again.

I needed to find my feet again, though, and went to see my old friend Hufnagel, from the Ferdinandshof army stables. The stables, with its horses, had switched from the Stettin area to Kleverhof, near Bad Schwartau. When I came into the courtyard, the first person I ran into was a well-fed individual. He was a Polish Feldwebel. At first I thought, 'I don't believe this'; for the Pole spread out his arms and cried, 'Good friend, good friend – Poland is not yet lost . . .' And as he embraced me, I suddenly realised who it was; he was the leader of the Polish band on which I'd managed to put some gentle pressure to play the Polish national anthem, a request which got me into such hot water afterwards. 'Noch ist Polen nicht verloren . . .'. One comes across everyone twice in one's life.

Goethe wrote these lines:

> 'The Gods, the blessed immortals,
> Give everything to those they love.
> Every joy the immortals give,
> Every sorrow; yes, everything.'

I can confirm that.

Postscript

A summary of Teddy Suhren's post-war career, by Helmut Herzig, President of the Teddy Suhren Marinekameradschaft, Zweibrücken

THE BRITISH PUT TEDDY SUHREN first in the POW camp, and then in prison. There he learnt that his parents and sisters had perished in the Sudetenland. That was a turning point in Teddy Suhren's life. On 12 April 1946 he was released, and as transport organiser took a freighter from Norway to England. The ship was stuffed full of women and children, and released soldiers with Norwegian wives. His orders on the ship were ignored; he himself had to clean the blocked toilets on board.

He stayed for a while on an estate at Bad Schwartau. The property was divided up, and he got 16 acres. Out of the savings from his service pay he bought himself a caravan and a cow. He made contact with his wife, daughter of a staff-officer in the Luftwaffe, whom he had married in 1943. He found her in Allgaü with her mother. She was working as a waitress in an American officers' mess, and in the meantime had acquired an American boyfriend. That struck Teddy Suhren like a hammer-blow. Many of those who returned home experienced similar tragedies.

Disappointed, Teddy Suhren returned to Bad Schwartau, where he experienced another setback. They had not reckoned with his returning, and had divided up his land. He left for Kiel, sold a silver-fox fur coat of his wife's to a member of the naval staff, and set up his 'Schnapps Factory' in a garden shed on the edge of town in Kiel.

There he distilled 38% black rum from sugar. Another ex-naval seaman sold filtered 'Torpedo-Spirit'. The police got a tip-off, but friends warned Teddy Suhren. In 1946 schnapps was more valuable than Reichsmark notes, and was just as valuable as cigarettes and butter. His business flourishing, he also began to butcher for the black-market. Shortly before the police moved in, he destroyed his still, and took himself off back to the estate in Schwartau where his caravan was still standing. He often helped with the sheep-shearing.

In summer 1947 his brother found a job for him: Suhren was to revive the broken-down merchant-shipping oil industry for an international mineral-oil concern. Suhren bought a 350 BMW for 850 Reichsmarks from the English occupation forces and rattled off to Hamburg. There another barrier arose; he had no movement authorisation, nor any work permit for Hamburg. At the labour office in Hamburg he ran into a Herr Klein, who recognised him and who once had sailed under Suhren, when he was still a 1WO. Klein helped Suhren where he could, and Suhren became manager at the mineral oil business in Hamburg. Later he was really successful in the industry. He helped many of his former fellow-servicemen in whatever way he could.

His former wife went off to the USA, but they never lost contact completely. Suhren married again, lived in Bad Dietzenbach (Hessen) and in Hamburg, and had three children with his wife Hannelore. Teddy Suhren refused offers to re-join the navy; he would not serve any state where servicemen were looked down on as murderers. Teddy Suhren was one of those who re-started the German Naval Association (DMB). On 31 May 1953 he was appointed Founding Chairman of the DMB at a big naval meeting in Wilhelmshaven, and spoke before 20,000 former fellow-members of the navy on the Town Square at Wilhelmshaven.

Teddy Suhren died on 25 January 1984 in Hamburg. He had already been terminally ill for quite a while. After his death his ashes were, as he wished, buried at sea in the place where his men from *U-564* had lain quietly on the seabed since 1 June 1943. (NW Cape Ortegal) 44 deg. 17′ North, 10 deg. 17′ West.

Appendix

Speech at the First Post-War Reunion of U-boat men, Hamburg, 1954, as published afterwards in the souvenir booklet of the reunion

. . . The next speaker is the former Führer of North Sea U-boats, Fregattenkapitän (retd) Reinhard Suhren, Wearer of the Knight's Cross with Oak Leaves and Swords, President of the U-Boot-Kameradschaft Hamburg.

Dear U-boat men –

There are a number of reasons why we are gathered together here today. Let me name three.

First there is the comradeship that we came to experience during our years together on the U-boats.

It is between nine and fifteen years since we finished with our community on-board, and perhaps kept in touch with each other by letter, but have not met up again since then – and how many friendships were formed then in the various prisoner-of-war camps. When the time of liberation was concluded, it was for many also the last time that they were together. Scattered all over Germany it was purely for financial reasons impossible for them to visit each other. So the desire was increasingly expressed by all ranks to arrange a reunion.

Here in Hamburg exists a U-boat Association.

In it U-boat men of both the First and the Second World War have found themselves together. This U-boat association has taken over the organisation and arranged this reunion with a good deal of hard work. The best outcome of all this work would be for good old links to be forged again, and if everyone were to leave this meeting with the feeling that he had been previously a member of a *bona fide* and honourable community of men, and could go on belonging to this community.

It is good that it is right here in Hamburg that you have gathered together from the entire Republic.

Hamburg is our most important seaport. You can well imagine with what urgency this port has been rebuilt. You can already find here again moving shipping, and see new and modern ships bearing the German flag. Our German merchant navy is being built up with enormous financial effort. We started in 1948 with only 136,000 GRT; but this rose to 202,000 in 1949, in 1950 to 610,000, 1951 to 1,115,000, in 1952 to 1,441,000 and in 1953 to 1,872,000 GRT. As former seafarers you will be particularly delighted with this development. If we did not already possess a merchant navy, we would have a right to establish one, for our task should be this: to look after our overseas trade, without which we Germans could not exist, and should it happen that our sea-routes were cut off, to struggle to clear them. Here in Hamburg you should consider how important for us to nurture this concept of the sea.

One other point, which will of course resound through our whole re-union, is this: to express *our regret over the absence of our two Großadmirals*, for we should not forget, as a comrade writes from Africa, that they belong to us, and sit there in Spandau on behalf of every one of us. We must leave it to the politicians to effect a change in circumstances for our two Großadmirals. We are certainly delighted that a first step has been taken, but the outcome is not enough for us. As former soldiers we ask the soldiers of the victorious nation to continue to make representations to their governments, and to say to them that we as former members of the German Kriegsmarine cannot understand why the two Großadmirals are still being held like alleged war-criminals under lock and key.

Let me glance back:

I came myself to the U-boat arm in 1938. For the first time I got to know this close ship-board community. It was still peacetime. What did we then absorb from the FdU, Kapitän Dönitz? His view was that we had a duty to the German people not to spare ourselves, but to make the U-boat arm strong through strenuous training, so that the resources devoted to it by the people would be in case of an emergency turned to account 100 per cent. In a surprisingly short period of time he succeeded in turning into reality his concept of a new kind of U-boat operation, and working to a scheme that would ensure complete success in the event of war. Quicker than we in the navy could have imagined, the war then came.

We as individual boats were not unprepared; we had gone through hard training, but as a navy or as the U-boat arm as a whole we were totally unprepared for a superior enemy, led astray by men who took advantage of the traditional political subordination of the soldiery. Though even then in the war we were soon in a position of not being politically hindered from running a war suited to the U-boat, nevertheless it was laughable how few boats were able to operate at the Front against the enemy, and how abandoned we felt as we launched out with two, three or even four boats into the mighty Atlantic!

We few men were supposed to pin down the sea traffic of the enemy in the West! All of the U-boat men in positions of responsibility at the time were clear about the impossibility of the task, despite which we did our duty and achieved successes which one would never have expected from this little unit. Then, as more boats were making an appearance a lot of costly time was lost and the enemy turned this to account by developing a lethal defence against us – radar.

To sum up, what was achieved in the way of bravery by the young men on the U-boats was pretty unique. How difficult it

Suhren addresses the 1954 reunion of U-boat men in Hamburg

became from this moment on for Großadmiral Dönitz to continue to send men against the enemy, can only be judged by one who has himself been put into the position of having to send them off. To have to give young men orders to go into action when their chances are slim is the hardest thing that can be demanded from men with a heart.

In two hard and terrible world wars German men have fought in a German U-boat service. At the end of the war, conquered, we have had to surrender our weapons. As the most highly respected U-boat leader in the First World War, Admiral

Bauer, wrote to me, his men refused nothing, but achieved tremendous things. I need to warmly greet you and say to you that in the First World War the U-boat arm went aground because it was wrongly in awe of the politicians during the war. Our Großadmiral Dönitz expressed himself absolutely clearly when he said that the men of the U-boat arm in the Second World War exhibited an unsurpassable heroism. We know today that it was false politics which involved us in this war too, especially in a war in which we had to oppose a superiority in materiel that we could not cope with. I consider it vital to underline that absolutely clearly in this company.

As we went on, we were at that time in no position to form a proper political picture. Only one belief was important to us: to serve our country as best we could with our operations. And this conviction gave us the strength to hold out to the last. We all had this belief, from the BdU right down to the youngest stoker, and it was this belief that linked the two of them. The spirit of comradeship, the spirit of absolute devotion of officers to men and vice versa, that was our spirit. This unique community was Dönitz's wish, and he was our example. Let no one in the world believe that Großadmiral Dönitz was not devoted to every single one of his kommandants and crews; and there is no question that he, like ourselves, acted from the best motives. It is impossible to conceive how difficult the spiritual burden for him now in Spandau must be, once he, like ourselves, realised that he had been deceived.

Then came the capitulation, and suddenly a propaganda machine was erected against us that we were completely unprepared to face. We were looked down on as despicable militarists, despite the fact that we had no idea at all even what a 'militarist' was. Everything that previously had been high and sacred was suddenly supposed to be the worst thing in the world. The instigators of this propaganda did themselves a disservice. We completely shut ourselves away from it at that time, in the face of it and every influence from it. We behaved in the proper way that men such a situation should do, we looked for a job in the ruins of Germany, the very best job we could, and started work. Of course we had learnt on our boats, when they were disintegrating under depth charges, that in those circumstances there is only one thing to do: to hang on tight, to tidy things up, and to repair what was broken, so as to become viable again.

Today we are able to say with great pride, that this approach, this getting down to work, was the right thing to do. As the German economy will bear witness, we became absorbed in the rebuilding process, and became recognised and valued colleagues in that work. There is scarcely a single former U-boat man who does not already have again firm ground under his feet. The fact that such a high percentage of the number of former U-boat men have gathered together is witness to this; for such a meeting is always linked to expense, and we have for a while not exactly been lying on a bed of roses in Germany.

As the situation in Germany consolidated, we ventured to concern ourselves with the past again to get a proper perspective as far as possible of the time which we found it so difficult to go through. I myself have become slowly but increasingly convinced that we fell victim to wrongdoing. That is painful to contemplate, but only if one looks at things objectively and also confesses this to oneself, can one take part in working towards the future. But even if we admit that we fell into wrongdoing, that does not exclude the fact that we at that time acted in good faith, and that was good. This is how we have guarded against spiritual conflicts, which otherwise would have led us to doubt our own human and personal worth. We have consciously kept ourselves clear of political discussions. We had quite enough to do with our work.

We live today in a democracy which we serve. We have to concern ourselves with political questions, each one with his personal opinion which expresses itself for most of us at the ballot box. We are clear about the fact that in a healthy democracy there is a government and a opposition. If we get actively involved in politics, may I offer you a bit of advice, specifically not to forget two things that we have learnt.

Officers and crew in convivial mood at the reunion.

The first is Tolerance.

On our boats we got to know each other pretty well, cooped up together in the most confined of spaces. The kommandant could not conceal his weaknesses from the youngest stoker, and vice versa, and it was those individual weaknesses which were aggravated by living together. But we managed to find a way of tolerating these weaknesses then, and to find a way of living together, and indeed that is the task in public life today.

The second point is Unselfishness . . .

When we were in the middle of a fight with a convoy, and we finally, for example, had fired our torpedoes, we stayed with it, in order to split up the defence and in order to keep contact with it and to summon other boats. We firmly believed that a united action could only be successful through the unselfishness of each separate boat. If we transfer these hard learned virtues today into political life, absolutely in the same way, whether we support the government or the opposition the usefulness of our young democracy will increase from it.

Apart from that we have learnt something else besides tolerance and unselfishness, which is worth mentioning. We have learnt to have respect for the work of other people. You will all remember being pursued by depth charges, when we heard these terrible bombs of destruction exploding at 100 or 200 metres. Then we were dependent on fate – and on the work of those who had forged our weapon back at home for us! And what those steel tubes put up with . . .!

When we then returned to the dockyard, it was not a hollow propaganda exercise but absolutely genuine when we shook hands with the dockyard workers. We who were proud of our decorations stood there thankful of the achievements of these men, who often after a night of terrible bombing took it for granted that they did their duty in their workplace. Drab in their work-clothes, no medals to recognise their importance; perhaps they had only just lost their family under the rubble. At that time all social distinctions were obliterated. If you are looking for something positive to take away from that terrible time, then this is it. I believe that I can say of us U-boat men, and I believe I can say for our generation, 'No one can win us over any more with the jargon of "class-struggle"!'

Perhaps there will be men who, because we are meeting up here again, class us as 'war enthusiasts' or similar. To them I can only say, 'Had we not known war, we would not have wished for it: today, now we know it, there is no way that we would wish for it.' People who try to foist the opposite onto us can only be malicious or stupid.

We often hear now that soon the need to 'play soldiers' should go away again. Now for any nation that decides to attend to its defence is certainly not a game but a damned serious problem. It means that the nation has provided itself with a moral and economic living-standard that seems to make life sufficiently worth living for it to be prepared to defend it. That is both a costly and very serious matter. But only he who has nothing to defend will therefore renounce the desire to defend himself. Dear U-boat men, my personal opinion is that any war that were to break out would be disastrous for the German people. There is only one thing worth striving for, and that is a long-lasting and undisturbed peace. The politician who manages to achieve that for us, will have done quite well enough, and we can only pray to God that He blesses the men who control the destiny of the people with judgement and ingenuity so that we can stay clear of that most terrible of all terrors, war. If atom bombs have any benefit at all, it can only be this; to make it clear to all those responsible, who might perhaps carelessly intend to start a war, that there is no bunker in the world where they cannot be hit, and they need to believe that as well. If the atom bomb disseminates this fear before any war, then it may be worthwhile – otherwise it is the most satanic invention ever devised.

We in the navy may be reproached for going on about the question of the defence of the Republic. It is not my task to explain why here. Nor is it my task to explain whether there is resentment when we feel solidarity with our Großadmirals. We have lived with our BdU, so I need waste no words on that. You all knew him and have seen him, and there can be no more accurate picture drawn than Wolfgang Frank does in his book.

Großadmiral Raeder was less well known to you. I myself was fortunate enough to get to know him personally. I should like to tell you a couple of purely human things: I remember a day in January 1942. I had come out of the HQ and was next invited to breakfast by Großadmiral Raeder. Time 14.00 hrs ! Lehmann-Willenbrock and I had arrived in Berlin the previous evening. I said: 'Hey, you warrior, look here, that is a particularly courteous breakfast-time for us ! It will give us a few more hours under the blankets!' So off we marched and made the most of it. The whole of Berlin got clouded over. About 6.00 am we shut the Jockey Bar from inside and then carried on. We didn't get a great deal of sleep.

Then at 14.00 hrs breakfast started. The admiral's staff smirked near us, and our ObdM kept gasping for air so as not to be completely overcome by the fumes. We were sitting not too far from him. Later, during a conversation over coffee and cognac, I could see, when the ObdM was discussing non-functioning torpedoes with me, how he was trying to go into reverse in order to extricate himself from my alcoholic cloud. When around 16.00 he excused himself and left his admirals to it, we all – you, Herr Admiral Rogge, will I'm sure still remember it – sat down cozily round the table, and among other things negotiated my promotion to Kapitänleutnant, since the admirals were moaning that no one could receive accelerated promotion in the navy, and that that needed to be changed.

The next day I was supposed to get my U-boat badge with diamonds, and then the promotion was supposed to be announced by the ObdM. I did indeed receive the U-boat badge, but no promotion, and as I left the room of the ObdM, I met Admiral Backenköhler, who congratulated me on my promotion. I said, 'No promotion. It didn't work out.' I had just about got to the bottom of the grand staircase nearby when Kapitän Freiwald summoned me back, coat-tails flying. The ObdM said to me, 'Now you must submit to something else; I promote you to Kapitänleutnant.'

Behind him grinned Admiral Schulte-Montig, beside me Freiwald. I stood there and could hardly restrain a smile, and my face must have been even more stupid looking than usual, so that the ObdM, who had noticed this but wasn't *au fait* with the situation, asked me, 'Well, don't you believe me? It's my prerogative; I can do it.'

And another occasion: it was autumn of the same year. I was invited to breakfast, again at 14.00. This time I came up to Berlin on the overnight train. In the proper naval manner I appeared at 13.55 in the Kaiserhof. There I met the Obdm already there and said, apologetically so to speak, 'Oh Großadmiral, are you here already?' Whereupon he replied with a laugh, 'Yes, yes, and you without a trail of exhaust fumes today!'

We had a great talk together. I didn't have the feeling that I speaking with the ObdM but with a very fine character and a warm-hearted comrade. Who in the world will get me to believe that this man is a war-criminal? He is not, any more than our BdU is. *We can compromise over many things, but not over this!* And one last thing I still have on my heart – *we bear no hatred towards the men who were our enemies at sea during the hard years of the war.* A fair war was waged by both sides. We want to make that absolutely clear – and today, my comrades, we don't want to hear any talk or songs which might offend our former opponents.

In this vein may I wish you – and myself – a happy time at this our first meeting after the Second World War.

Index